T0161728

Praise for *Plant Teachers*

"A wonderful book, comprehensive and concise, bridging cultures at a time when we need it the most. Jeremy Narby, this time with the help of Rafael Chanchari Pizuri, invites science back to the dance — to learn, laugh, and remember."

— JOSEPH TAFUR, MD, author of *The Fellowship of the River: A Medical Doctor's Exploration into Traditional Amazonian Plant Medicine*

"*Plant Teachers* offers a rare glimpse into the worldview of a Peruvian healer, Rafael Chanchari Pizuri. Anthropologist Jeremy Narby is our guide, bridging Western science with traditional knowledge, traversing this gap delicately and respectfully. The first chapter describes the indigenous belief that certain plant species have an 'owner' or 'mother' — 'something like a personality' — and that it is possible to learn from that other-than-human source. This book presents an opportunity for Westerners to stretch their concept of reality and enter into the magical depths of the Amazonian jungle, a wholly different kind of learning."

— RACHEL HARRIS, author of *Listening to Ayahuasca: New Hope for Depression, Addiction, PTSD, and Anxiety*

"Tobacco is the preeminent medicine plant of the Americas, yet few anthropologists have ever paid attention to it. This book may be the first to take a serious and respectful look at the spiritual role of tobacco in an indigenous culture. Half of the book is about ayahuasca, and it makes a valuable contribution to ayahuasca literature, offering insights from the Shawi culture and a discussion of ayahuasca pharmacology that is one of the most thorough, up-to-date, and readable I have seen. But what makes this book stand out — indeed, what make it unique — is its treatment of the subject of tobacco. By juxtaposing ayahuasca and tobacco as plant teachers, this book conveys that tobacco is to be taken as seriously as ayahuasca. *Plant Teachers* may open the door to a new way of looking at tobacco."

— GAYLE HIGHPINE, linguist and author of "Unraveling the Mystery of the Origin of Ayahuasca"

"Jeremy Narby's interest in validating indigenous knowledge in the light of science is long-standing. Here, he juxtaposes interviews, evidence-based debunking of misconceptions about tobacco, and reconsidering of assumptions on DMT-enhanced ayahuasca to bring forth productive insights. Rafael Chanchari Pizuri's views are informed by both his ancestral tradition and his acquaintance with biomedicine: he is clearly a cross-cultural knowledge seeker. Socratic exchanges on local understandings of ecology in an animist worldview open a small but irresistible window into the complexity of Amazonian shamanic plant knowledge. Are the hornworms, who prey on tobacco plants, pests or valued 'spirit owners' or both? Not merely a reductionist match between science and a Shawi shaman's perceptions, this reference-packed little book leads the reader to a refreshing, open-ended questioning. By intertwining his and Chanchari's 'pursuits of knowledge' in dialogue, Jeremy Narby successfully de-exoticizes both Amazonian shamanic and possible global therapeutic uses of tobacco and ayahuasca, bringing them closer together."

— FRANÇOISE BARBIRA FREEDMAN, affiliated lecturer in the department of social anthropology, University of Cambridge

"Jeremy Narby likes to pry into life's mysteries, and in *Plant Teachers* he and coauthor Rafael Chanchari Pizuri carry on that noble pursuit with excellence. Taking on the challenging topic of tobacco as sacred medicine, they manage to make sense of it all in a manner exceeding what others have tried. Much of the book is a conversation between the authors. Rafael, a Shawi indigenous man and *médico* from Peru, offers experienced advice and unique insights into the discussion of the plants and their uses. He is wonderfully down-to-earth and straightforward. The long elucidation of ayahuasca is very finely done, and the book packs in a huge number of references. This is a fine piece of work. Bravo!"

— CHRIS KILHAM, medicine hunter

"Once again the brilliant advocate of 'bi-cognitive' consciousness, with his usual crystalline clarity and scalpel-sharp precision, Jeremy Narby continues his unique lifelong exploration of how the tension between scientific and shamanic paths to knowledge can trigger penetrating new insights. In dialogue with his deeply informed, profoundly sophisticated interlocutor, Shawi healer Rafael Chanchari Pizuri, Jeremy dives into rarely discussed aspects of traditional Amazonian plant usage and the most updated scientific research on the topic, offering a much-needed corrective in a field recently deluged with far too many half-baked, overly romanticized takes on shamanism."

— J. P. HARPIGNIES, author of *Delusions of Normality* and *Animal Encounters* and editor of *Visionary Plant Consciousness*

"Jeremy Narby has done it again. This is just the book that is needed in these times: a bridge between indigenous knowledge and Western science that is both rigorous and accessible. Narby has deep respect from both ways of knowing and masterfully reconciles them together into a holistic perspective that is bigger than the sum of its parts. A tour de force for anyone interested in the world of plant teachers, ayahuasca, or tobacco."

— JERÓNIMO MAZARRASA, the International Center for Ethnobotanical Education, Research, and Service (ICEERS)

PLANT
TEACHERS

PLANT TEACHERS

AYAHUASCA, TOBACCO,
—————— *and the* ——————
PURSUIT of KNOWLEDGE

Jeremy Narby *with*
Rafael Chanchari Pizuri

Foreword by Gayle Highpine

New World Library
Novato, California

New World Library
14 Pamaron Way
Novato, California 94949

Text design by Tracy Cunningham and Tona Pearce Myers
Illustrations on pages 9, 37, and 55 © Yvonne Byers; illustration on page 19 © Shutterstock.com

Library of Congress Cataloging-in-Publication Data

Names: Narby, Jeremy, author. | Pizuri, Rafael Chanchari, author.
Title: Plant teachers : ayahuasca, tobacco, and the pursuit of knowledge / Jeremy Narby, with Rafael Chanchari Pizuri.
Other titles: Ayahuasca, tobacco, and the pursuit of knowledge.
Description: Novato, California : New World Library, [2021] | Includes bibliographical references and index. | Summary: "A western anthropologist and an indigenous Peruvian shaman hold a cross-cultural dialogue about the similarities between tobacco and the hallucinogen ayahuasca and the role these substances both play in the cultures of the indigenous peoples of the Amazon region"-- Provided by publisher.
Identifiers: LCCN 2021021168 (print) | LCCN 2021021169 (ebook) | ISBN 9781608687732 (hardcover) | ISBN 9781608687749 (epub)
Subjects: LCSH: Indians of South America--Drug use--Peru. | Indians of South America--Tobacco use--Peru. | Ayahuasca--Physiological effect--Peru. | Tobacco--Physiological effect--Peru. | Traditional medicine--Peru. | Traditional medicine--Amazon River Valley. | Ethnopharmacology--Peru. | Ethnopharmacology--Amazon River Valley.
Classification: LCC F3429.3.D79 N37 2021 (print) | LCC F3429.3.D79 (ebook) | DDC 615.3/2369--dc23
LC record available at https://lccn.loc.gov/2021021168
LC ebook record available at https://lccn.loc.gov/2021021169

First printing, August 2021
ISBN 978-1-60868-773-2
Ebook ISBN 978-1-60868-774-9
Printed in the USA on 30% postconsumer-waste recycled paper

New World Library is proud to be a Gold Certified Environmentally Responsible Publisher. Publisher certification awarded by Green Press Initiative.

10   9   8   7   6   5   4   3   2   1

CONTENTS

FOREWORD

This book makes a valuable contribution to ayahuasca literature. But what makes it stand out — indeed, what makes it
unique — is its treatment of the subject of tobacco.

Tobacco is the preeminent medicine plant of the Americas.
Every other medicinal or entheogenic plant is used only in particular regions, but tobacco is used in every part of Native America — North, Central, South, and Caribbean.

Yet tobacco is barely noted by anthropologists. An anthropologist working with the Achuar in the Ecuadorean Amazon
was gathering information about their medicinal plants, till he
realized that he never saw anyone actually *using* any of those
plants when they were ill. For every illness, they used tobacco.
So he just lost interest in their medicinal plant use. Like most

anthropologists in the Amazon, he didn't care to find out more about tobacco.[1]

Some writers, like Johannes Wilbert, in his book *Tobacco and Shamanism in South America*, hint that the shamanic use of tobacco may be only a cover for nicotine addiction. Indeed, Wilbert almost seems to suggest that, in South America, shamanism itself may be just a pretext for consuming tobacco, in absurd quantities, by every possible route.[2] But that notion ignores the fact that not all shamanic use of tobacco even requires ingestion. In fact, in some North American cultures, tobacco is traditionally not ingested at all. At least, not by humans.

Among North American Indians, like my own ancestral Ktunaxa people, tobacco is considered food for the spirits. Tobacco can be sprinkled or thrown into a fire to amplify prayers. During gatherings, tobacco is offered to other plants to say thanks and to repay the plants for their help by strengthening the spirits of the plants with the power of tobacco.

Tobacco is offered by those requesting help from the spirits. A pinch of tobacco can be placed at the base of a tree with a prayer for the tree's help, much in the same way that a pouch of tobacco is offered to a medicine person to solicit their help.

Tobacco smoke can be blown onto a person or object to protect it or strengthen it. It is used to feed the energies of protection, like feeding watchdogs to keep them strong. Tobacco is like a megaphone for our prayers.

None of this uses smoking. Even in the Pipe Ceremony, tobacco is not inhaled, but taken only into the mouth and blown out as an offering.

Traditionally, tobacco was sometimes smoked in solitary or

communal meditation, but never carelessly or disrespectfully, while doing other things.

The spirits can absorb the energy of tobacco only if there is human intent to give it to them. If some tobacco just fell at the base of a tree and rotted there, it would not feed the spirit of the tree. Tobacco is an amplifier of our intent.

As such, if tobacco is *grown and processed and offered* with the intent of addicting people and making money, it will carry that intent as well. And, as we all know, when used carelessly, unconsciously, and disrespectfully, tobacco can sicken and kill people.

But even commercial tobacco, grown with base intent and adulterated with chemicals, can be offered to the spirits. So few people offer tobacco to the spirits nowadays, it is said, that the spirits are starved for it, and if you're starving, you don't turn up your nose at food even if it's junk food.

In hidden corners of reservations, medicine people still cultivate sacred tobacco. Some use seeds passed down from the old days in a lineage never used for anything but sacred purposes. They sing to the tobacco as it is growing and imbue the tobacco with their songs.

Tobacco has been cultivated in North America everywhere it would grow and traded where it wouldn't. It was likely the first plant ever cultivated in the Americas. Even peoples who didn't practice seed agriculture for food cultivated tobacco (proving that people who followed a hunter-gatherer way of life didn't do so out of ignorance about seeds). Tobacco Plains, Montana, is named for the rich tobacco gardens of the Ktunaxa people.

But the tobacco cultivated there was neither *Nicotiana tabacum* nor *Nicotiana rustica*, originally cultivated in eastern and southwestern North America, respectively, and familiar to us, respectively, as cigarette tobacco and *mapacho*, or shamanic tobacco. (Both species originate in South America and appear to be anthropogenic.) The species most used by Native peoples in western North America outside the Southwest was *Nicotiana quadrivalvis*, which is low in nicotine, and in the Southwest, *Nicotiana attenuata* was also cultivated. When commercial tobacco was introduced, many people found it too strong for smoking, so they mixed it with kinnikinnick or red willow bark. This again contradicts the notion that the sacred use of tobacco is merely a cover for nicotine addiction.

So does the fact that when tobacco was brought to Siberia, the Native shamans recognized its power and adopted it for shamanic use. It was introduced by the Russians for recreational use, probably in the 1600s, and many of their people took up recreational smoking. But the shamans sensed its real purpose.[3] When tobacco reached Mongolia, the shamans there adopted it as well.

Some Native American people say, only half tongue-in-cheek, that the reason humans were placed on Earth was to cultivate tobacco for the spirits, because the spirits cannot do it for themselves. When I came to the Amazon, I was startled to hear indigenous people say the same thing.

I was also startled to hear that Amazonian shamans drink tobacco tea. Nicotine is more lethal, per weight of dosage, than arsenic or cyanide, and drinking or eating tobacco can be fatal. Surely, I thought, the tobacco tea they drink must be very weak.

But I didn't hear much about that practice — until a friend of mine apprenticed to a *yachak*, or shaman, of the Napo Runa people in Ecuador. My friend thought he was apprenticing to become an *ayahuasquero*, or ayahuasca shaman. But once he had committed himself, the "secret" of ayahuasca healing was revealed to him: tobacco. "Ayahuasca only helps you *see* the work that needs to be done," the *yachak* told him. "Tobacco gives you the power to actually *do* it."

It's not enough to *perceive* the spirit world; one must be able to *affect* it as well. Anyone can drink ayahuasca, and local people would often try to cure their own ailments by drinking ayahuasca themselves before heading to the professional *ayahuasquero*, like trying home remedies before going to the doctor. When they turned to the *ayahuasquero*, it was because he could *do* something. And that ability came from the power of tobacco.

Tobacco is the "muscle" of the work. A *curandero*, or healer, has to do battle in the spirit world. So he has to build up his inner *soldados*, or soldiers. That requires drinking tobacco — *Nicotiana rustica*, which is very high in nicotine.

My friend was given small quantities of tobacco to eat daily, and once or twice a week he had to drink tobacco tea, which made him sick and miserable. I once participated in a tobacco drinking ritual myself and discovered how he felt. My body knew it had been poisoned. Vomiting gave no relief from the nausea, because the nausea didn't come from the gut, but from the brain — like seasickness. One experience of drinking tobacco was enough for me. I did continue to take nasal infusions of tobacco tea, though. It was invigorating to feel small doses of the poison trickle down my throat. But my friend had to drink tobacco over and over, in ever-stronger doses, for months.

Tobacco is related to the *Datura* genus. It is a cousin of

brugmansia (aka *toé*, wanduk, and angel's trumpet), jimson weed, belladonna, and mandrake — plants that, like tobacco, draw their power from their closeness to the world of death.

As a poison, nicotine works on the nervous system. But drunk in gradually increasing doses, it creates a tolerance, and that tolerance is permanent. Which means that it creates some sort of permanent change in the nervous system.

Like many Amazonian peoples, the Napo Runa have the same word for "medicine" and "poison," *hambi*. By being poisoned and surviving, my friend came out changed. Tobacco was no longer deadly to him. He could drink doses that would kill a normal human. He could now walk unscathed to the doorway of death.

He found the visionary realm of tobacco to be distinct from that of any other entheogen. But visions were not the main reason he was made to drink tobacco. Lots of plants give visions. The reason an apprentice *ayahuasquero* has to drink tobacco is its power. Very experienced tobacco shamans develop the ability to drink an unlimited quantity of tobacco without harm. But learning to command that power is another task.

This book gives us a glimpse of the tobacco practices of other Amazonian cultures, the Shawi and the Asháninka. While there are differences, the profound respect for tobacco is the same.

By juxtaposing ayahuasca and tobacco as plant teachers, this book conveys that tobacco is to be taken as seriously and treated with as much respect as ayahuasca. That makes this book unique in the growing literature about ayahuasca and Amazonian shamanism.

— Gayle Highpine, linguist and author of
"Unraveling the Mystery of the Origin of Ayahuasca"

INTRODUCTION

My first brush with tobacco as a plant teacher occurred back in 1985, when I was living in a community of Asháninka people in the Peruvian Amazon. These were people who thought that plants like tobacco and ayahuasca could impart knowledge to those who consumed them; and in their view, tobacco was the number one plant teacher. When Asháninka people had a problem or an ailment, they would consult the *seripiari*, meaning "tobacco shaman" in their language.

For my part, I had no particular affinity with cigarettes or cigars, nor did I think one could learn much by smoking them. I grew up with a father who was an ex-chain-smoker turned zealous anti-smoker and a mother who only smoked outdoors, as if in hiding, and I viewed smoking tobacco as an unhealthy waste of time. As a young anthropologist, I was interested in understanding the views of indigenous Amazonian people. And truth be told, I was fresh out of the university library.

As the months went by in this indigenous community, a man named Carlos Perez Shuma became my main interlocutor. He was forty-five years old and happened to be a tobacco shaman. We would talk in Spanish for hours, and he would tell stories about his life, many of which involved tobacco: how his uncle taught him to use it when he was young; how it protected him from dangers and enemies of all sorts; how it attracted invisible beings called *maninkari* that animate all living beings. One day, after witnessing Carlos Perez blow tobacco smoke on a sick baby that someone had brought over for a healing session, I asked him how tobacco could help in such cases.

He replied, "I always say, the property of tobacco is that it shows me the reality of things. I can see things as they are. And it gets rid of all the pains."

Some of the stories Carlos Perez told about tobacco defied my understanding of reality — but I figured my job as an anthropologist was not to express skepticism but to record the person's point of view in their own words, and to ask questions if I did not understand. On one occasion, he told me about the demise of his father-in-law, who was a renowned tobacco shaman: "He used to drink his tobacco like it was water; he would pick it up and drink it like this, as if it was nothing. And then he could do what he wanted to. Better yet, he would transform into a jaguar in front of everybody."

"Really?" I asked.

"That's why they killed him, because he often turned into a jaguar and attacked cattle," he continued.

"Attacked cattle?" I asked, not sure I had understood correctly.

"Attacked cattle," he replied.

"Whose cattle?"

"The colonists'."

"Why did he attack their cattle?"

"Because he wanted to mess with them. So they killed the jaguar, and took out the heart and cooked it with ashes, resin, and hot peppers. And as my father-in-law's soul itself had gone outside of him and was in the jaguar, this gave him a shock. That's why he died — not from illness, but he died in his soul."

"So the colonists killed him?"

"No, the colonists owned the cattle, but they hired some Asháninkas to kill the jaguar. Because if a real jaguar attacks cattle you can shoot it and kill it. But if it has the soul of a tobacco shaman, you can shoot it from up close and it can still leap, and even though you shoot from over there, you can't kill it, because it's people ["*porque es gente*"]."

"So how did they manage to kill the soul of your father-in-law?"

"Because they betrayed him. As the jaguar's heart was being cooked, my father-in-law was telling us that he had already escaped three times. He said, 'I don't know how I will die, because many people want to kill me, but they won't be able to.' Maybe there came a time when he could no longer dodge; maybe they used something secret, and he gave up his body, and they sucked out his soul. That's how he died. Because he died fat and healthy."

"Healthy?" I asked.

"Healthy. And at the moment of his death, there was a burning smell of gunpowder. That's why he said, 'They've got me now.

It seems as if I can no longer live, because in truth they cooked my heart, so I don't have life.' At his death, he was dripping, as if they had drenched him in water. His sweat was flowing because they put his heart in the fire; that's why it burned. And so that's how it was."

As Carlos Perez told me this story, I realized that I did not think the events it related were possible. As a child of rationalism and materialism, I did not think a person's soul could fly out of their body propelled by a strong dose of tobacco, lodge itself in a living jaguar, and get stuck there to the point of causing the person's death, once the physical jaguar's heart had been cut out and cooked in chili peppers. Nor did I really know what to do with such a story.

After a year living in this Asháninka community, I accompanied Carlos Perez on a visit to his old tobacco shaman teacher, who lived up in the hills about an hour's walk away. The man seemed at least eighty years old, as he was all covered in wrinkles, but Carlos Perez told me that no one knew his exact age because he was born before Asháninka people started counting years, probably in the early years of the twentieth century. He was sitting on a mat, wearing a cotton gown and eating tobacco paste from a small stick that fit into a gourd.

When I was introduced, he looked at me with a glint in his eye and asked whether I was his father-in-law. I wasn't even a third his age at that point, so this was clearly a joke. I decided to play along with the old man and answered yes. He laughed and asked me again, "*Konki* [father-in-law]?" "Yes," I replied. He asked me the same question about twenty times in a row. Each time, I answered yes, and his laughing got a little longer.

(Later that day I learned from Carlos Perez that the question also meant, "Can I have sexual access to your daughters?" — so the joke was on me.)

I put an end to our exchange by asking if I could try some of his tobacco paste. He handed me the gourd, and I put a good stick's worth between my lips and then sat to the side to allow the two men to discuss their business. After a short while sitting there, thinking about nothing much, I ran my tongue under my front teeth, and they seemed to be particularly long and sharp. And my face seemed to have cat whiskers growing out the side that allowed me to sense the environment more sharply. My mouth tasted of blood, and though I was a vegetarian, I enjoyed the taste. My senses were telling me that I was turning into a feline. This wasn't the kind of thing I thought possible, but the impression seemed real. This feline sensation made me feel warm, powerful, and wise. I eyed some chickens that were clucking about nearby, and like a benevolent jaguar, decided *not* to pounce on them. I remember telling myself, "You know the tobacco paste is strong when the anthropologist starts attacking the chickens!"

This feline and predatory impression, which lasted about half an hour and then faded into a feeling of calm and clarity, was so vivid that it remains with me to this day. But it took a long time before I felt able to discuss it in public.

The years slipped by after this experience, and I kept a distance from tobacco. It was not a plant that called me — fortunately, because I knew its regular use could harm human health.

Nevertheless, I continued to respect the plant because

indigenous Amazonian people insisted on its central role, and because I valued my brief encounter with it. Sensing with my body what it might feel like to be a jaguar was an experience I was grateful to have had — but not one I was eager to repeat.

I did not think that I had really transformed into a jaguar in any measurable way. Rather I had an intense, body-based memory of the impression of "being a feline" that I could tap into at will and use as a source of strength and courage.

But I learned not to talk about this with Westerners, because the subject seemed to make people uneasy. Even a basic discussion of the Amazonian perspective on tobacco tended to cause incomprehension. People would remind me that tobacco use caused millions of smokers to die prematurely every year, and international health authorities called it "the most preventable cause of death in the world today" — so how could anybody consider the plant as a source of knowledge and healing?

It seemed clear to me that the Western view was based on an understanding of the effects of manufactured cigarettes, which offered an adulterated version of the plant, most often laced with industrial chemicals. And it also seemed clear that indigenous Amazonian people had know-how about tobacco that could perhaps be useful to the world's smokers and to people seeking to understand this powerful plant. But there was a gulf between the two worlds that remained hard to bridge.

The years continued to tick by. In 2010, Carlos Perez Shuma passed away. For a long spell after that, I could hardly look at the transcripts of the interviews we did together. He had been a person of knowledge and a master storyteller, and I missed him dearly.

In 2018, thirty-three years after my initial brush with Amazonian tobacco, I felt a calling to return to the subject. No specific event triggered this; it happened more like a ripe fruit falling from a tree. Suddenly I knew that I wanted to look into the Amazonian perspective on tobacco.

I contacted Rafael Chanchari Pizuri, an indigenous expert on the matter and an elder of the Shawi people. He works near Iquitos, in the Peruvian Amazon, where he teaches young indigenous teachers in training. He also describes himself as a *médico*, a Spanish word for "doctor" or "healer" used locally to refer to specialists who heal people with indigenous medicine. Tobacco plays an important role in his practice.

I told Rafael Chanchari that I was interested in trying to outline the proper way of approaching this powerful plant teacher. I had interviewed him several times previously, and he readily agreed to share his knowledge, replying, "Tobacco is an important medicinal plant, and its deeper meaning depends on how one uses it." We met in Iquitos, and our ensuing conversation about tobacco is the subject of chapter 1. I audio-recorded our dialogue in Spanish, and then translated it into English.

Several months later, I began delving into the recent science of tobacco. My goal in bringing science into the discussion was not to validate or invalidate Amazonian knowledge but to juxtapose the two points of view and see how they lined up next to each other. I charted my inquiry into the scientific literature on the different points made by Rafael Chanchari — and, to my astonishment, found considerable correspondences between indigenous knowledge and contemporary science. This is the subject of chapter 2.

At that point, it became clear that Rafael Chanchari and I had going a nascent research project that combined two ways of knowing and that afforded a more complete understanding of a powerful and often dangerous plant. I suggested that we follow the same procedure and turn our attention to another psychoactive plant from South America, the ayahuasca vine. This plant had only recently sprung to fame, for better and for worse. It forms the basis of a vegetal brew that bears its name, which some consider to be a potential remedy for depression, trauma, anxiety, and addictive behaviors and a tool for personal exploration and growth; and which others view as a dangerous hallucinogen.

Rafael Chanchari has ample experience working with ayahuasca, which he uses alongside tobacco in his practice as a *médico*. Almost a year after our initial dialogue, we met again, this time to discuss ayahuasca. This exchange is the subject of chapter 3.

After these conversations about tobacco and ayahuasca, Rafael Chanchari and I agreed to do a short book together that would give both the indigenous and scientific angles on the two plants.

As I had with tobacco, I explored the recent scientific literature on ayahuasca, guided by Rafael Chanchari's understanding, and found that the Amazonian point of view helped me make sense of a new domain of scientific research. This is the subject of chapter 4.

As coauthors, we both view science and indigenous knowledge as complementing each other, despite certain differences. By bringing them together, our first goal is to allow them to exist side by side. In this way, readers may consider both and draw their own conclusions.

This book has two authors, deals with two plants, and brings together two systems of knowledge. We hope you enjoy it.

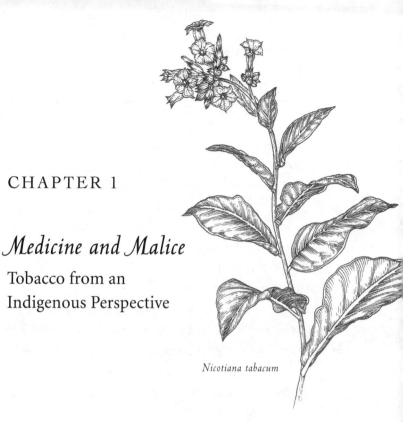

CHAPTER 1

Medicine and Malice
Tobacco from an Indigenous Perspective

Nicotiana tabacum

L ate one morning, Rafael Chanchari and I met at the school where he teaches. He is a relatively small man in his fifties with a kindly air. We sat in a quiet room, and I turned on the recorder.

Amazonian people often refer to the "owner," or "mother," of an individual species — something like a personality — so I began by asking Rafael Chanchari if Shawi people speak of an "owner" of tobacco.

"Yes, we Shawi people say, *pinshi wa'yan*, meaning the soul or spirit of tobacco; and *pinshi a'shin*, meaning the mother of tobacco, the one who discovered it or the one who invented it, the one who sowed it for the first time. This mother is the caterpillar man — *kuntan*, as we say. This caterpillar has a scientific name;

I saw it on the internet. So this is the mother, according to our culture."

He spoke with a soft voice and pronounced each word distinctly. "The mother is a man?" I asked.

"A man," he replied, agreeing. "But transformed. It's a whole story. Tobacco has a soul, it has a spirit, which is of two sorts, medicine and malice [*maldad*], or what we call in Spanish sorcery [*brujería*]. It has two spirits."

"Do all plants have two spirits, or just tobacco?"

"All the plants that have power — in other words, the teacher plants: ayahuasca, tobacco, *toé*, *catahua*, chambira palm — have two spirits or two souls. So the person who works with these plants must choose to learn medicine or malice. And the spirits of these plants offer you this choice because they are not small-minded. Sometimes they want to teach you both. But it is the person who chooses."

To get a better understanding of the "mother" of tobacco, I asked Rafael Chanchari if he had ever seen this entity during his work with teacher plants.

"Yes," he replied, "but I didn't see the mother; I saw her soul."

"But what is the difference between the *soul*, the *spirit*, and the *mother* of a plant?" I asked.

"In the Shawi language, all beings — such as trees, fishes, birds, mammals, and reptiles — have souls, or mothers. But in Spanish I hear there is a difference between 'soul' [*alma*] and 'spirit' [*espíritu*]; they say that persons have souls, while plants and animals have spirits. That's why I sometimes use the word *spirit* to refer to the souls of plants. The soul or spirit of a plant is an entity specific to that plant. Whereas the mother of a plant is specific to its species."

As a bilingual person, Rafael Chanchari thought about the world in his mother tongue, Shawi, and when he expressed himself in his second language, Spanish, he took liberties with it; even though he knew that Spanish reserved the word *soul* for humans, he used it anyway to refer to plants and animals, because he saw no fundamental difference between the souls of humans and those of other species. He is what anthropologists call an animist — in other words, someone who considers all living beings as subjects or persons.

He went on to explain that there were two main types of tobacco — one with thick double leaves, the other with small thin leaves — and one could use both to make *mapacho*, or shamanic tobacco. "The one with the double leaves is stronger. One supposes that it contains a greater quantity of natural chemical substances for seeing visions."

This prompted me to ask if he thought there was a connection between nicotine and the mother of tobacco.

"Clearly, nicotine is what activates our neurons in a way that allows us to perceive the imperceptible in our visions and dreams," he replied. "That's how we can detect that plants have spirit. The spirit is the image of the plant in the world of visions. The mother is a being both physical and spiritual. Caterpillars are the mother of tobacco, and they have a spirit that can teach you."

Rafael Chanchari saw no contradiction between plant mothers and spirits on one hand, and neurons and molecules on the other. In his view, perceiving the mother of tobacco required nicotine and neurons. His approach included science, which helped the dialogue between us.

"And do you work with tobacco?" I asked.

"Yes, I smoke."

"So, when you see the soul of this plant, what does it look like?"

"Look, these two kinds of tobacco I'm telling you about, if you prepare them by adding a quantity of ingredients from other forest plants that have power, this makes it powerful, and it teaches you medicine, or it teaches you sorcery. And about its soul, I have seen it. It is gigantic and masculine — a tall brown man, the same color as tobacco. That is the soul of tobacco, the one who teaches you."

"And when you see this tall brown man, does this entity make you feel fear? Or is it agreeable, or enchanting? What is tobacco's personality like?"

"As a being, it does not give a feeling of fear. You can be in its presence. It only imparts fear because it teaches malice. That is its line; that is the line of prepared tobacco."

Rafael Chanchari seemed to suggest that tobacco had something like a political agenda, or a party line. But before I could query him about this, he went on to explain how to make "prepared tobacco." First, one must protect the young tobacco plant from the green caterpillar that seeks it out as food.

"Is this the same caterpillar as the mother of the plant?" I asked.

"Yes, and if you let it be and you don't take care of your plant, the caterpillar will eat it all. It's a real disgrace, but for the caterpillar, tobacco is its food."

He said that once the healthy tobacco leaves turn yellow, one harvests and dries them. This is *mapacho* in its simple form. But to produce prepared tobacco, one first has to make a paste by cooking the central veins of the dried leaves with different plants, including ginger, cinnamon, vanilla, the giant vine *clavo huasca*, and the aromatic vine *sacha camote*. One boils this mixture down to a paste, allows it to cool, and spreads it on the dried *mapacho* leaves, which one then rolls together and dries again. "And this is the prepared tobacco that teaches you sorcery. In the old days, my people used to have it prepared like this — now they do it less and less. They used to cure it, then smoke it; they dedicated themselves to this and practiced this.

"Earlier you asked me what tobacco's soul or personality is like," he said, referring back to the "tall brown man" he'd mentioned before. "Well, he doesn't frighten you, but what happens is that he wants to teach you malice. In other words, in the spiritual world, in the forest, in the water, there are strong spirits that can harm you, and this tobacco wants to teach you this."

"Why does it want to teach this, in your opinion?"

"Let's say that it is an activity for the spirits of the plants. Just as medicine is an activity, and curing and healing bring satisfaction, for the plants it is the same: malice is an activity that they carry out for their own satisfaction. But for human beings, malice is painful, unsatisfactory, and difficult. The power of these plants can cause human losses. This is their mission: to teach us to practice their activities according to their line, to cause harm. Piercing the human body in a way that causes loss of life is an activity for them. And conversely, medicine is also an activity that we develop, to heal, give life, and make life longer. And tobacco itself does indeed make life longer, because it cures you. Simple *mapacho* tobacco, like what they sell in the market of Belen [the large outdoor market in Iquitos], can be used for medicine, and you can smoke it just like it is."

"If tobacco is a medicine, which illnesses does it cure?" I asked.

"Tobacco takes away drowsiness, and it cures incompetence and laziness in people and in dogs. Around here, we talk of people who live 'in the easy' — people who make no effort to learn the skills needed to produce the food they eat to stay alive. Tobacco can cure this. It can also cure people who, out of sheer laziness, don't know how to do things. More generally, it serves to transfer power, capacities, and abilities, but this requires *icaros* [curing songs/chants] for the teachings to have an effect. Tobacco also helps heal snakebite and the bite of stinging ants. And it strengthens the masculine and feminine hormones. And when added to other anticarcinogenic plants, it potentiates them."

"So why does it cause cancer among cigarette smokers?"

"Traditional consumers of tobacco did not suffer from lung cancer or mouth cancer. But consumers of 'fine' cigarettes get cancer, because they consume in excess and without guidelines. In life, all things used in excess are harmful. Smoke is not suited to human consumption. In small doses, tobacco smoke is medicinal, but in abundance it destroys the cells and deteriorates the organism."

We sat in silence for a moment. Rafael Chanchari's words seemed precise and coherent.

Before I could formulate another question, he resumed discussing the uses of tobacco: "With tobacco smoke, you can heal fright. And it serves to scare off snakes and keep them at a distance. It also keeps away river dolphins. It does the same with bad spirits in ayahuasca sessions. For all these things one can use tobacco, as well as for healing people who no longer know how to hunt and fish. Tobacco allows you to have an exchange with *sacharuna* ["forest person" or "forest people" in Quechua]. If you want to be in touch with *sacharuna* because you want to ask him to give up his birds and animals so that you can hunt, you place a *mapacho* cigarette on a large branch of a *lupuna* tree, because that is his home."

Some of Rafael Chanchari's statements could be approached scientifically — for example, by consulting the scientific liter- ature on the impact of tobacco use on sex hormones. Others, such as the existence of the invisible forest being *sacharuna*, could not, at least for the time being. But I did not want this to become an obstacle in our conversation; in an intercultural dialogue such as the one we were having, basic politeness con- sisted in considering the other person's point of view. If Rafael Chanchari felt comfortable discussing nicotine and neurons, I too should feel comfortable discussing the "mother of tobacco" and *sacharuna* the forest person.

People in Western Amazonia widely regard *sacharuna* as the "boss of the forest." But anthropologists have noted that discus- sions about this entity are often evasive; as Peter Gow put it: "It is never very clear whether *sacharuna* is one spirit for all the forest, or many spirits each with a particular area."[1] I found it intriguing that an ambiguous and invisible entity such as *sacharuna* should appreciate tobacco. But I left the matter in the air because I had some practical questions to put to Rafael Chanchari.

I asked if he had any advice for the many people around

the world who smoke cigarettes, which contain a weak form of tobacco that is quite different from the Amazonian kind.

"Yes. Look, my advice would be for all of humanity. It is okay to consume simple tobacco, rolled-up tobacco leaves. Even the stronger tobacco can be used, but only in the evenings before going to sleep, because it teaches you to dream good things. So, in the evenings, after a meal, two or three rolled cigarettes can be used in order to sleep. That would be my advice: moderately consume two or three rolled cigarettes before sleeping and after dinner. But not during the day, no. Too much smoke also has consequences, like anemia, because inhaling smoke is not that good for the health; it is not very nutritional for the human body."

"And do you ever smoke cigarettes that come in packets?" I asked.

"No, I don't smoke those. Because one time, I didn't have any *mapacho*, and I didn't have any money to buy any. And I went to drink ayahuasca at a session near Nauta, and nobody there had *mapacho* either. And my friends said, 'Here are some *Caribe* cigarettes. Let's smoke them.' So I smoked *Caribe*, and the ayahuasca said to me, 'This cigarette is not good for drinking ayahuasca. It is not good for human beings.' It said to me, 'It is garbage, simply garbage.' Tobacco is a complement to the medicine. Tobacco is medicine."

"Ayahuasca told you the cigarette was garbage?" I asked, wanting to be sure I had understood correctly.

"Yes, ayahuasca said the tobacco in industrial packets is garbage. 'That is garbage. You are smoking garbage.' That's why it punished me, because I was smoking —"

"How did it punish you?" I asked, interrupting him.

"By sending me very strong visions, a sensation of death — in this sense it punished me. So it told me that this tobacco was garbage, it wasn't worth it. When you drink ayahuasca, you need *mapacho* to complement the medicine."

I commented that most regular tobacco users in the world smoked cigarettes that he would probably consider garbage. Then I asked if he had any advice for people who might want to get to know tobacco better.

"I would advise that before smoking any industrial cigarette, it would be better to obtain simple, normal tobacco. It doesn't need to be the strong, prepared kind. And you can moderately smoke up to three of these in the evening in order to sleep. This tobacco also helps to stabilize oneself if one is excited, when there is too much emotion, or when depression sometimes comes, or anger."

"And if people are going to smoke simple tobacco, how should they smoke?" I asked. "Should they stand up or sit down? Should they smoke alone? Do you have a point of view on this?"

"Yes. It is important to have a special place for smoking, because not everybody can tolerate breathing tobacco smoke; people's noses are not prepared for it — some are allergic, others have sinusitis — and it is important to respect the health of other people. So you have to look for a space where you don't scare other people, where three or four people can smoke, sitting down, concentrated. Nor should you watch television, because this activity enchants you. So smoke and concentrate; think about what you are doing. That would be the advice: only smoke where there are no people who do not smoke, because it would affect their noses. And stop doing other activities — dedicate yourself exclusively to smoking *mapacho*. Because it is a plant that has power, that has spirit, or soul. So it is important to respect this. It is not just an ordinary thing that you are smoking. That would be the advice I would give."

Nicotiana rustica

CHAPTER 2

Remedy and Poison
The Science of Tobacco

Scientists have studied tobacco more than any other plant in the history of science. This is because of its natural chemical complexity. The tobacco plant produces about four thousand different organic substances — not to be confused with the hundreds of industrial chemicals that cigarette manufacturers add to their products.[1]

In particular, tobacco produces a number of substances called alkaloids, which contain nitrogen and have strong physiological impacts on animals and humans. Nicotine is by far the primary alkaloid contained in most of the 76 documented tobacco varieties, including both species commonly used in the Amazon, *Nicotiana tabacum* and *Nicotiana rustica*. It is one of the more toxic botanical substances in nature, as one or two drops of pure nicotine placed on the tongue or skin can kill an adult human.[2]

From the plant's point of view, nicotine serves first and foremost as a defense against predatory insects. This role is so effective that people have used nicotine as a potent insecticide for centuries.[3]

In some varieties of *Nicotiana rustica*, the nicotine content of the leaves approaches 20 percent — whereas the blond tobacco used in industrial cigarettes contains between 1 and 2 percent. Since a couple of drops of pure nicotine is a lethal dose, consuming powerful dark tobacco can be a risky undertaking.[4]

The toxicity of nicotine depends on how it enters the body. When absorbed through the skin, it is about one thousand times more potent than when eaten or smoked. When one eats tobacco, stomach acids break down the nicotine molecule to some extent. And when one smokes it, the high temperature of the combustion transforms a large part of the nicotine into less lethal compounds. Chemists Penny Cameron Le Couteur and Jay Burreson comment, "This does not mean tobacco smoking is harmless, just that if this oxidation of most of the nicotine and other tobacco alkaloids did not occur, smoking would invariably be fatal with only a few cigarettes."[5]

The fact that industrial cigarettes contain hundreds of chemical additives, which turn into new and considerably more toxic substances when burned, is another matter. Combustion is only good news for smokers inasmuch as it reduces the lethality of the nicotine contained in tobacco.[6]

Smoking is a fast way of getting nicotine into the blood and brain, with relatively little risk of overdose — smoking too much strong tobacco tends to make people nauseous, or even unconscious, and so they tend to stop smoking before reaching a fatal level of nicotine intoxication. It turns out that smoking is by far the most common way that Amazonian shamans consume tobacco — though they also chew, drink, lick, and snuff it, as well as, in rare cases, consume it through rectal absorption.[7]

Ethnobotanist Dale Pendell comments on the dangers of absorbing tobacco in liquid form or through the rectum: "Drinking, if the initiate does not vomit up the tobacco after losing consciousness, may result in death or permanent injury. The most hazardous technique of ingesting tobacco is the tobacco enema [rectal injection], wherein the danger of overdose is extreme."[8]

NICOTINE'S WORKINGS IN THE BODY

To grasp the full power of tobacco, it helps to understand the workings of nicotine inside the human body.

Nicotine has a profound impact on people because the nicotine molecule resembles an important chemical produced by our bodies and brains called acetylcholine (pronounced "uh-see-tuhl-KOH-leen"). This allows nicotine to fit into the receptors for this substance on the surface of neurons and of many other cells in the body. These receptors are commonly known as *nicotinic receptors*, because they were discovered in the early twentieth century by scientists seeking to understand how nicotine functioned in the body. When nicotine binds to our neurons, it causes them to release a flood of brain chemicals, such as dopamine, glutamate, noradrenaline, and endorphins, as well as acetylcholine itself. These brain chemicals go on to have a wide range of effects.[9]

For example, increased dopamine activates the reward center in the brain, which makes people feel pleased and also reinforces their desire to repeat the experience — hence the addictive potential of nicotine; increased glutamate strengthens connections between neurons, which facilitates learning and remembering; increased endorphins, which are small proteins that function as painkillers, can lead to feelings of euphoria; and increased acetylcholine makes people feel alert and reenergized. Nicotine can trigger all these effects at once via its impact on brain receptors designed for acetylcholine.[10]

But acetylcholine is not just a brain chemical. Many brainless organisms throughout nature produce it, including bacteria, unicells, moss, algae, and primitive plants. This indicates that it appeared very early in the evolutionary process. Acetylcholine is an "extremely old molecule" involved in regulating basic cellular functions, like gene expression, cell proliferation and differentiation, cell-to-cell contact, immune function, electrical activity, locomotion, secretion, and absorption. The vast majority of human cells produce acetylcholine and have receptors for it on their surfaces. There are nicotinic receptors on cells in muscles, the skin, the pancreas, the lungs, the pituitary gland, the adrenal glands, the immune system, the digestive system, blood, the ovaries, and the testes. This allows nicotine to have an impact all over the body, including the cardiovascular, respiratory, renal, and reproductive systems.[11]

People who consume tobacco feel some of nicotine's effects. For example, when nicotine stimulates adrenal glands to release adrenaline, a hormone that increases heart rate and blood pressure, consumers can feel this "rush." But nicotine has numerous subtle effects on the body that escape the awareness of tobacco consumers. For example, it promotes the growth of new blood vessels, and it quiets inflammation when the immune system overreacts.[12]

As cardiologist John P. Cooke put it, nicotine "is much like fire — it can be very harmful, and yet it can be useful if you know how to control it." For example, promoting the growth of new blood vessels makes tumors grow faster, so consuming nicotine is a bad idea if you have cancer; but if you have diabetes, and your extremities suffer from poor blood circulation, applying a topical nicotine gel to them may help reverse the trend.[13]

Likewise, the chronic intake of nicotine weakens the immune system — which partially explains why cigarette smokers have a higher incidence of disease than nonsmokers — but when the immune system overreacts, as it does in severe cases of Covid-19, for example, nicotine seems to have protective effects. Initial reports that cigarette smokers seemed to develop less severe forms of this viral illness — which have since become the subject of scientific controversy — led a team of researchers to consider that Covid-19 might affect nicotinic receptors; they went on to identify a toxin-like sequence of amino acids in one of the virus's proteins that is similar to a sequence found in snake venom proteins, which block nicotinic receptors and prevent the action of acetylcholine. One of the many roles played by acetylcholine is to act as an anti-inflammatory molecule, in particular in cases when the immune system overreacts and floods the body with pro-inflammatory molecules. Normally, in such cases, acetylcholine neutralizes these pro-inflammatory molecules. But if the nicotinic receptors are blocked, no acetylcholine is released and the pro-inflammatory molecules go on to attack healthy cells throughout the body, which eventually causes the lungs to fill with liquid and other organs to shut down. When this happens, patients end up dying from their immune response to the virus, rather than from the virus itself. Though the evidence is still contested and inconclusive, it is possible that in its most severe form, Covid-19 is a disease of the nicotinic system, and in particular of the acetylcholine-based anti-inflammatory system; and nicotine may restore the function of this system by allowing acetylcholine to suppress the immune system's overreaction.[14] The scientists testing this hypothesis work with "medicinal nicotine" in the form of transdermal patches or nicotine chewing gum, and unanimously warn that smoking cigarettes or vaping nicotine products affords no protection against this aggressive viral illness.[15]

Nicotinic receptors also play a role in the development of Parkinson's disease, Alzheimer's disease, schizophrenia, and epilepsy. Accumulating evidence suggests that nicotine may be of therapeutic value in Parkinson's, an illness that kills dopamine-producing neurons, because nicotine stimulates dopamine production in the brain. Nicotine also helps with Alzheimer's, an illness that produces plaque deposits between neurons, because nicotine prevents the proteins that form these deposits from joining together. Nicotine may also help people suffering from schizophrenia, but the exact mechanism of its action remains unclear in this case. Finally, people suffering from epilepsy should avoid consuming nicotine, as it can trigger seizures.[16]

NICOTINE AS PAINKILLER, COGNITION ENHANCER, AND HORMONAL AGENT

Ample evidence shows that tobacco can function as a painkiller and, as Rafael Chanchari says, help soothe snakebites and the bites of stinging ants. Amazonian people have long treated ailing and painful parts of the body with wet tobacco leaves or tobacco powder plasters — which function like organic nicotine patches. Scientists recognize that nicotine reduces pain by acting on the nicotinic receptors of nerve cells in the brain and the spinal cord. Morphine works, at least in part, by releasing acetylcholine, which acts on these same receptors. Research suggests that low doses of nicotine, administered by patch or nasal spray to people who do not smoke, reduces their need for morphine after a surgical operation. It also suggests that people who smoke tobacco or consume nicotine on a regular basis end up desensitizing their nicotinic receptors and develop a tolerance to nicotine's effects; and for this reason, they do not benefit as much as irregular consumers do from its painkilling effect.[17]

There is also solid evidence that, as Rafael Chanchari noted, tobacco can help people learn. Scientists confirm that nicotine can improve attention and memory. It increases cerebral blood flow; it releases glutamate, which strengthens connections between neurons; it releases noradrenaline, which focuses attention; and it activates areas in the forebrain thought to underlie cognition. In the words of psychologist Marcello Spinella: "Nicotine, the principal psychoactive alkaloid in tobacco, has cognitive-enhancing effects."[18]

Research also confirms Rafael Chanchari's assertion that

tobacco "strengthens the masculine and feminine hormones" — though this effect depends on how one uses the plant. Urologist Wei Wang and colleagues studied a large sample of men and found that smokers have more total testosterone and free testosterone than nonsmokers. They also found that the nature of the effect depended on the regularity of consumption: "Smoking can lead to an acute increase in testosterone levels, but this can decrease with chronic exposure to tobacco by long-term smoking. Therefore, the effects of smoking on testosterone levels depend on personal smoking history." Another study found higher levels of testosterone and estrogen in men who smoke compared to those who do not.[19]

Epidemiologist Judith S. Brand and colleagues studied a large sample of postmenopausal women and found that cigarette smoking increased their levels of estrogen, as well as their levels of testosterone, "with the highest levels being observed among those smoking the most cigarettes."[20] However, they noted that estrogen levels were highest in heavy smokers, but women smoking fewer than ten cigarettes per day had lower levels of estrogen than nonsmokers.

Research shows that women have more difficulty giving up smoking than men and experience more intense cravings; they are also more sensitive than men to the rewarding effects of nicotine. In 2017, neurobiologist Sara Cross and colleagues wrote, "Preclinical research has predominantly focused on adult males. … As a result, the exact mechanisms underlying females' unique sensitivity to the effects of nicotine are poorly understood." However, they suggest a possible explanation: "There is some evidence for interactions between circulating hormones or menstrual cycle phase with smoking behavior and cessation success. In women, estrogen seems to promote smoking behavior." Concretely, women tend to smoke more at the beginning of their menstrual cycle than they do at the end.[21] More research is needed on the unique sensitivity of women to the effects of nicotine.

TOBACCO AS HALLUCINOGEN — AND MEDICINE

Rafael Chanchari refers to tobacco as containing "natural chemical substances for seeing visions." Until recently, scientists did not consider nicotine, or tobacco, as a hallucinogen. But those who are knowledgeable of the high doses of strong dark tobacco consumed by Amazonian shamans recognize the plant's potential to generate hallucinations, or visions. As anthropologist Johannes Wilbert put it: "There remains no doubt that nicotine through action on the central nervous system is capable of producing hallucinatory eschatological scenarios on a cosmic scale and the question remains whether these effects are caused by the nicotine alkaloid directly and/or indirectly through the interaction with neurotransmitters other than acetylcholine."[22]

Nicotine may cause some of tobacco's hallucinatory effects by its capacity to release brain chemicals such as noradrenaline and serotonin, both of which are chemically related to hallucinogens (mescaline and psilocybin, respectively).

Moreover, several studies have found small amounts of the alkaloids harman and norharman in tobacco smoke, but not in tobacco itself, suggesting that these compounds are created during combustion. As they are both closely related to the hallucinogenic harmala alkaloids found in the ayahuasca vine, they may contribute to the hallucinatory effects of tobacco. Nevertheless, the neurological mechanisms involved in shamanic tobacco's capacity to generate hallucinations remain unclear. Currently, most academics familiar with the subject consider nicotine to be the compound that triggers tobacco visions.[23]

In the words of anthropologist Christian Rätsch: "The effects of tobacco are primarily the result of the nicotine. Low dosages of tobacco produce invigorating and stimulating effects that suppress feelings of hunger. Moderate dosages can easily result in nausea, vomiting, diarrhea, anemia, and dizziness. High dosages can lead to delirium with hallucinations ... and to death due to respiratory paralysis."[24]

Anthropologist Martin Fortier recently categorized hallucinogens used in ritual context according to the brain receptors they affect. In one category, he placed psilocybin mushrooms, ayahuasca, peyote, and the San Pedro cactus, which stimulate serotonin receptors. In a second category, he placed datura, deadly nightshade, mandrake, and brugmansia (*toé*), which block nicotinic receptors, causing delirium and intense hallucinations. In a third category, he placed tobacco: "Several classes of substances are both atypical and weakly hallucinogenic (that is to say hallucinogenic only at very high doses). The most important of these substances is tobacco, which derives its hallucinogenic effects by stimulating nicotinic acetylcholine receptors. Different species of *Nicotiana* particularly concentrated in nicotine — and which therefore induce visions — have held a central place in Amer-indian cultures."[25]

There is a growing consensus that strong dark tobacco can function as a hallucinogen and induce visions in those who consume it.

Like Rafael Chanchari, other Amazonian people tend to view tobacco as a *medicine*. The anthropological literature abounds with statements to this effect. For the Huni Kuin people in Brazil, tobacco is "the quintessential healing substance." For the Matsigenka people in Peru, "tobacco is a medicine in the fullest sense." More generally speaking, tobacco "is the shamanic plant par excellence in South America ... without which no shamanic activity can take place." Blowing tobacco smoke on a patient or applying tobacco juice to the part of the body that appears to be suffering is "the most common healing practice ... in the whole Amazonian region."[26]

However, it is important to note that Amazonian people tend not to make a radical distinction between "medicine" and "poison." Some Amazonian languages use the same word to refer to both concepts.[27] Amazonian people commonly seek out bitter, pungent, or toxic plants to use as medicines. From their perspective, tobacco fits the bill as both a toxic plant and a medicinal one; as Rafael Chanchari says, tobacco has two souls, one for medicine, the other for malice.

This aligns with the ambiguity of the first known uses of the term *pharmakon*, from which we get the words *pharmacy*, *pharmaceutics*, and *pharmacology*. In ancient Greek, *pharmakon* can refer to a remedy or a poison. Paracelsus famously made this point by distinguishing poison and cure by dose: "The dose makes the poison," as the adage goes.[28]

Contemporary scientific research certainly confirms this ambiguity, showing that tobacco and nicotine have healing potential, and can also cause harm and death. They are medicine/poison.

FRICTIONS BETWEEN SCIENTIFIC AND INDIGENOUS VIEWS

Many of Rafael Chanchari's assertions about tobacco have scientific backing. But some seem less amenable to a scientific reading, at least at first glance.

Consider the concept of plant teachers. Anthropologist Luis Eduardo Luna first brought attention to this notion in his 1984 study of mestizo shamans in the Peruvian Amazon, writing, "Among them there are those called *vegetalistas* or plant specialists and who use a series of plants called doctors or plant teachers. It is their belief that if they fulfill certain conditions of isolation and follow a prescribed diet, these plants are able to 'teach' them how to diagnose and cure illnesses, how to perform other shamanic tasks, usually through magic melodies or *icaros*, and how to use medicinal plants."[29]

Plant teachers are those that impart knowledge to people who consume them. In 2011, an international team of scientists identified fifty-five species considered "plant teachers" and used in shamanic initiation across the Peruvian Amazon, including tobacco, ayahuasca, brugmansia, datura, and coca, as well as several nonpsychotropic plant species with purgative, strengthening, or protective properties.[30]

Many scientists consider the "plant teacher" concept too

radical, because of its "implicit animistic roots," which "push the limits of academic orthodoxy."[31] But in the case of tobacco, the cognition-enhancing effects of nicotine offer a sufficient reason to rethink this view. Given that nicotine helps people focus, remember, and learn, the idea that nicotine-rich tobacco can act as a "plant teacher" comes into focus. The concept may still be a metaphor, but it reliably describes what goes on in our minds when we consume the plant.

At times, as one goes back and forth between Amazonian knowledge and science, one finds a lack of corresponding concepts. For example, Rafael Chanchari refers to "souls" and "spirits," whereas science has no place for such notions. But when Amazonian people refer to "souls" and "spirits," these terms do not have quite the same meaning as they do for Westerners. In Western thinking, these concepts are grounded in a fundamental opposition between body and soul, matter and spirit. But when Amazonian people refer to the invisible entities that animate living beings as "spirits," they do not conceive of them as fundamentally immaterial; rather, they see these beings as essential to the organisms they animate: when they leave, the organisms die. From an Amazonian perspective, what distinguishes these entities is not their immateriality but their invisibility.[32]

When asked to comment on this in an email exchange, Never Tuesta Cerrón, the director of the teacher-training program that employs Rafael Chanchari and a member of the indigenous Awajún people, replied:

> For many years, I have thought about how to translate into Spanish the conceptions that we indigenous people have about the soul or spirit of the

plants and animals that have been persons in the past. As Awajún people, when we want to explain our conceptions to mestizos, we use Spanish terms such as *alma* [soul] or *espíritu* [spirit]. In Awajún, we say "*wakani*." For example, to explain that a photo is an image of Dora, we say "Dora *wakani*"; to refer to Dora's shadow caused by sunlight, we say "Dora *wakani*"; to explain that we saw the soul of Dora, who died some time ago, we say "Dora *wakani*." Likewise, when we refer to the plant teachers who used to be persons in the past, we use the term *wakani*, for example, "*datema wakani*," meaning the soul or spirit of the ayahuasca plant. The problem I see is that our interlocutors understand *soul* or *spirit* in the religious sense. For us Awajún, we are clear that a plant or an animal that used to be a person in the past, has *wakani*.[33]

In response to this statement, Rafael Chanchari commented, "For us Shawi, it is the same, except that we say *wa'yan* rather than *wakani*."

Anthropologists Lewis Daly and Glenn H. Shepard recently discussed the concept of "soul" of the Matsigenka people of Peru in the following terms: "The Matsigenka word for spirit or soul, *suretsi*, also refers to the heartwood or pith of a plant.... *Suretsi* can refer to the pharmacological principles of medicinal and toxic plants. When a plant is heated in water, its soul 'contaminates' or 'infuses' the brew. When a person drinks the decoction, the soul of the plant, manifest in its taste, odor and coloration, 'infuses' the body with this holistic substance/soul."[34]

Since Amazonian people view souls and substances as synonymous while scientists make an absolute distinction between the two, going back and forth between science and indigenous knowledge can get tricky.[35]

Like many Amazonian people, Rafael Chanchari refers to the "mothers," or "owners," of plants — invisible entities specific to each species that are like a personality. Scientists have little time for this kind of personifying, given that their main method consists in doing the opposite and objectifying what they study. For science, "to know is to de-subjectify,"[36] as anthropologist Eduardo Viveiros de Castro put it. This means that a scientific perspective on the "mother of tobacco" will probably not be available anytime soon.

However, it is possible to take seriously the concepts of Amazonian people and find coherence. In 2010, anthropologist Françoise Barbira Freedman focused on the gendering of shamanic plants in the Peruvian Amazon, a subject that had been largely ignored until then. She found widespread agreement with Rafael Chanchari's assessment that the mother of tobacco is masculine. She writes, "The most inclusive level of gender complementarity of plants in Upper Amazon shamanism is that between tobacco and all other 'master plants.' Tobacco is considered to be the male catalyst that enhances the effects of all other shamanic plants. Lamista Quechua shamans frequently assert that tobacco is the 'father of all plants,' a male consort to the 'mother spirits' of all shamanic plants."[37]

Furthermore, considering living beings as persons, or subjects, does not necessarily preclude viewing them as objects.[38] Viewing tobacco as animated by a powerful and ambiguous personality does not contradict considering the plant as a sac full of alkaloids. In fact, these two views can complement each other. By personifying tobacco, the indigenous approach allows one to develop a relationship with the plant — and to put a face on the danger it embodies. As Rafael Chanchari says, tobacco can easily lead people astray, and working with this powerful plant requires knowledge, discipline, and concentration. Personifying tobacco may help people consume the plant in a less harmful and more constructive way. Helping smokers gain respect for the "mother of tobacco" may be just as productive as telling them to avoid smoking because nicotine is addictive and smoking causes cancer.

Ultimately, one's point of view on this matter depends on one's worldview. Those who wish to stick to an exclusively materialist position, and consider plants and animals as objects rather than subjects, can do so. And they might be interested to know that the caterpillar identified by Rafael Chanchari as the "mother of tobacco" is an actual insect known as the tobacco hornworm (*Manduca sexta*), which produces a specific protein called CYP6B46 that binds to nicotine and neutralizes it. This allows the caterpillar to munch on tobacco leaves with impunity; it also allows the animal to exhale nicotine-laden breath, which deters predatory spiders. This insect's mastery of nicotine is still not fully understood, though scientists have been looking into it for more than fifty years.[39] But the notion that *Manduca* somehow "owns" tobacco may seem less far-fetched once one knows about the molecular underpinnings of its mastery.

THE DANGERS OF TOBACCO

Finally, a health warning. Tobacco is a dangerous plant to consume. Smoking industrial cigarettes harms nearly every organ in the body; causes many diseases, including numerous fatal forms of cancer; and reduces the health and lifespan of smokers. Even smoking unadulterated tobacco is not safe; as Rafael Chanchari says, "inhaling smoke is not that good for the health." Consuming tobacco in other forms is also harmful. For example, using electronic cigarettes to consume nicotine may eliminate the production of the carcinogenic by-products of combustion, but it presents its own specific toxicity issues; it also causes inflammation of the lungs, impairs their ability to fight off infections, and increases the risk of nicotine overdose and seizures. Even "medicinal nicotine," in the form of transdermal patches, chewing gum, or nasal sprays, can have serious side effects and lead to overdoses if used at the same time as smoking cigarettes. Chewing and sniffing tobacco come with their own risks (see the appendix for a detailed review of the health risks posed by vape, snuff, snus, and *rapé*). There is no entirely safe and riskless way of consuming tobacco or its main alkaloid, nicotine. Just handling green tobacco leaves can produce headaches, nausea, and vomiting, a form of poisoning known as green tobacco sickness.[40]

That's how it is with plant teachers. They are powerful, dangerous entities. One can establish alliances with them, and work with them prudently and respectfully, but one never masters them. At best, one can avoid being mastered by them.

With this little book, we do not wish to incite people to

consume tobacco, or ayahuasca, or any other psychotropic plant. Rather, we seek to encourage those who are interested in these powerful plants to find out more about the risks and opportunities they present.

Last but not least, we deplore the consumption of manufactured cigarettes, which offer a weakened version of a powerful plant teacher, most often laced with industrial chemicals. Cigarettes are a travesty of tobacco — to be avoided at all costs.

CHAPTER 3

Two-Sided Purge
Ayahuasca from an
Indigenous Perspective

Banisteriopsis caapi,
vine and cross section

Almost a year after our initial conversation about tobacco, Rafael Chanchari and I met once again, this time on a weekday evening in the courtyard of a hotel in Iquitos. He wore khaki pants and a white short-sleeved shirt with a couple of pens protruding from the front pocket. We sat down together at a quiet table. We were the only customers in the establishment. A creaky pedestal fan whirred nearby.

I began by saying that people in different countries had recently developed an interest in ayahuasca, and it seemed important that they have access to Amazonian voices on the subject. He nodded in agreement.

My first question concerned the ayahuasca vine itself, which botanists view as a single species (*Banisteriopsis caapi*), in contrast to Amazonian experts, who recognize a range of varieties. Referring to the different kinds of tobacco he had described in our initial conversation — some for healing, some for causing harm — I asked if it was the same with ayahuasca.

"Yes," he replied, "there are many varieties of ayahuasca — sky, thunder, *mariri* ["magical phlegm"], lightning — with different characteristics. You can tell them apart by their color; broadly speaking, there is black ayahuasca and yellow ayahuasca, but if you go into detail, there is a range. Yellow ayahuasca is called 'sky' [*cielo*]. '*Cielo* ayahuasca' is for medicine, for vision. That's what I drink, and in my garden I only plant sky, and not the other varieties, which teach malice and sorcery and all that; we don't drink that, but there are other people who do."

"Is it easy to see the difference between sky ayahuasca and black ayahuasca just by looking at the vines?"

"Sky ayahuasca is yellow when you scrape the vine, whereas black ayahuasca is dark in color. There are several types of black ayahuasca: thunder ayahuasca and *mariri* ayahuasca, and both vines have short knots on their main trunks. It is easy to distinguish between them by their color and shape."

"Is it dangerous for foreigners to drink ayahuasca without knowing about these differences?"

"Yes, it is dangerous; it is risky. I have an experience I can tell you about: I started taking ayahuasca on my own, because my grandfather was an *ayahuasquero* [ayahuasca shaman], and so was my uncle. So I began drinking, and then I met a teacher, Fermín Murayari Aguiler, whose father was Kukama and whose mother was Piro. He was a *médico*. I had the opportunity to spend a couple of weeks with him. I told him, 'Maestro, I want to learn.' He said, 'I'm going to teach you, but I will not be the one who teaches. Instead, the spirit of ayahuasca will study you and see what kind of person you are and whether you can learn. Then you will learn.'

"Maestro Fermín and I drank together about fifteen times. One night he scolded me for having drunk ayahuasca on my own: 'Why are you learning sorcery? This is not good, because you are going to kill children, and the parents will suffer. You are going to kill wives, and the husbands will suffer. You are going to kill men, and wives and children are going to suffer. And you will not have many years to live, because they will kill you. They will put a bullet in you.' As I listened to him, my head was spinning from ayahuasca. The next day, I asked him, 'Maestro, why did you say those things last night?' He replied, 'I said those things because I saw that you were learning sorcery.' I said, 'Maestro, my intention in taking ayahuasca on my own was not to learn sorcery, but to see visions, to know what ayahuasca is like deep down, in the spiritual world. That's why I drank, and that's why I'm drinking. Now that you say I'm learning sorcery I want you to clean me.' Maestro Fermín said, 'I will clean you. And we will continue drinking.'

"And in the following days, every time I drank, I sweated like never before. Usually, I never sweat. But during those days, I sweated a lot, and that's how he cleaned me up. As he did this, I went through a lot of tests; ayahuasca tends to test people who drink it. I felt fear. I could see the whole cosmic world, and it contained so much suffering that I found it discouraging. This was a test. I almost told my teacher that I was going to stop drinking, but then I decided to drink one last time, and if it did not go well,

I would stop there. And that night was the best. I no longer saw suffering; everything became transparent, clear, and calm. The spirit told me, 'Now put this into practice. Contact the people you want to be in touch with.' I remember calling a deceased sorcerer called Encarnación Yumi Tangoa. When I called his name mentally, he did not reply, but then I saw lights approaching, and behind them I heard him say, 'Why did you call me?' I replied, 'I am calling you because I am practicing how to contact people spiritually.' He said, 'Ah, very well. You are learning. Learn. This will help you be a man.' Then he left.

"I called other people too. Sometimes those who showed up threatened me: 'Why are you calling? You don't have the right to call me. You're interrupting the work I was doing. So now you are going to die.' I was afraid I was going to die, but Maestro Fermín had told me to defend myself. So I defended myself by saying, 'No, I don't have to die, because what harm did I do? None at all. I'm just checking my ability to contact you.' And the Maestro blew *mapacho* smoke on me and said, 'That is the way to make contact, and to defend yourself, and to see from afar.' This is how I learned to handle ayahuasca. So, for foreigners who come here to drink ayahuasca, it can be very dangerous. They can learn how to practice sorcery and how to harm people."

"What would you advise foreigners to do to avoid this danger?"

"Above all, they should ask what kind of ayahuasca they will be drinking. *Médicos* cannot lie. That's one of the things that ayahuasca tells you: don't deceive. You have to be honest, that's what ayahuasca says, and this means that you can't mislead people. If you are serving black ayahuasca, you have to tell people that it's black ayahuasca. And if it's yellow ayahuasca, which is sky, you have to tell them they are drinking sky ayahuasca. And foreigners should choose to drink sky ayahuasca."

I asked Rafael Chanchari about the risks of drinking ayahuasca mixed with *toé* (*Brugmansia suaveolens*), which is a dangerous datura-like plant occasionally added to brews prepared for foreigners who seek powerfully hallucinogenic experiences. "The effects of *toé* last a long time," he replied. "With *toé*, your head will spin for one or two days, even three days, sometimes a week. It is not good for a person to be in such a state for so long, drunk and in bad shape. It is not recommended for drinking; there is no advantage to doing so. And there are other people who mix *chiric sanango* [*Brunfelsia grandiflora*] into their ayahuasca, which brings dizziness and intense cold. This is dangerous. Personally, I do not like the cold; it has no value. One should not make people suffer like this. Some people do this because they want to experiment, but I would say that even that is not a good idea, because it makes for a cold dizziness, with cold sweat.

"Adding all kinds of different plants to ayahuasca will not make the brew stronger; instead, it will make the human body suffer, and that means taking risks. Perhaps this is why people have died on occasion. It is better to drink simple ayahuasca, which lasts four hours, after which you are normal again. Why put in so many things and take risks? If people have heart disease or high blood pressure or too much cholesterol, for them it is risky to drink ayahuasca mixed with other plants. It is better to drink the simple brew, ayahuasca mixed with chacruna [*Psychotria viridis*], or ayahuasca mixed with yagé [*Diplopterys cabrerana*]. I drink either one of those simple brews."[1]

"What's it like drinking ayahuasca made from the vine alone, without chacruna or yagé?" I asked.

"Drinking pure ayahuasca is a practice among the Wampis, Awajún, and Achuar peoples [indigenous people of the Peruvian and Ecuadorean Amazon]. They prepare pure ayahuasca and drink it, then they go to sleep in the forest in search of visions."

"Have you tried this?"

"One time I drank pure ayahuasca in Zungaro with an Awajún friend and some colleagues. I drank about eight cups, but I didn't vomit. And after that, I didn't want to drink any more because I was afraid something might happen. With the brews I am used to, one cup is usually enough to feel the effects. So I went to sleep, and then a spirit told me that I should have drunk at least four more cups if I had wanted to have visions and work as a healer. That's how it is among Awajún people; that's their practice. They take their young people to an isolated place in the forest to drink and then sleep; and sometimes in their dreams they meet those they call *arutam*, meaning 'spirits of the ancestors,' who transmit messages — for example, to become a warrior or a hard worker or a builder, or to live well and be a good person; those are the kinds of things they find in visions. But there are also individuals called *iwishin* who drink in order to cure illnesses; they do not drink to have visions, but to have medicinal visions, to heal. That's how it is among the Awajún."

"And when one drinks the vine alone, does one also have visions?"

"It makes you dream. When you are really dizzy from drinking, you go to sleep, and then you dream. Or some people choose to go into the forest, and the spirit guides them. And while they are walking, they feel a presence. For example, an Awajún friend told me that when he was in the forest after drinking pure ayahuasca, he was drunk, and he felt and saw what seemed like thunder strike him. That's what they call dreaming. And at that moment, he received a message, and his drunkenness disappeared."

"Was the message a voice?"

"Yes, it was a voice. But first, it was as if lightning had struck him, and there was thunder, and then he heard the message. For the Awajún, that is encountering visions."

"In your experience, is drinking the vine alone good for the health?"

"It's good for the health; it strengthens you and gives you visions. But it takes someone with experience to organize it, a *waimaku*, a practitioner who has had *arutam* visions. The person who harvests the ayahuasca has to fast; they cannot eat but can only smoke *mapacho*. Those who scrape and pound the vines, and those who gather the firewood for cooking them, must also fast. On the second day, they cook the ayahuasca in a cauldron. They cover the pounded vines with water, boil the liquid down to a third of its volume, separate it from the vines by pouring it into a separate cauldron, and continue to cook it down. Then they cover the vines with water for a second time and repeat the process. They spend the day cooking the ayahuasca in this way, fasting all the while. At nightfall, they go to the hut that they have built for the occasion and drink the ayahuasca. Then they lie down on their mats and go to sleep. The *waimaku* watches over them and sings to them. Those who have good dreams wake up and go walking on the path in the forest to find visions.

This is an important event for Awajún people, and it takes dedication to carry out. But we Shawi people do not practice this."

"How often do you drink ayahuasca?"

"Before, when I dedicated myself to studying ayahuasca, I would drink twice a week. But now I have a lot of work to do, so I only drink occasionally. When I was learning and drinking twice a week, I was very thin, and this is risky, because you are dieting and not eating nutritious food. I did this and found it very difficult. It's better to drink twice a month."

People in the Peruvian Amazon commonly refer to ayahuasca as *la purga*, "the purge," so I asked Rafael Chanchari if purging was an important part of the brew's medicinal effect.

"Yes, it cleans the stomach of all the impurities that we ingest with our food and drink. Look, when you want to purge, when you want to clean out your stomach in order to drink ayahuasca, you don't need to diet that much; you can eat and drink. And if you drink ayahuasca on a full stomach, within thirty minutes or so, you will vomit and go to the toilet, and this will clean you out, but it will not make you dizzy. And if you drink a brew made only from the leaves of the ayahuasca vine, this is magnificent for purging. It doesn't make you drunk, but it sends you to the bathroom for a total cleanse. It empties you."

"Is this good for the health?"

"Clearly, because it cleans your stomach and intestines. One time I went to the hospital to check if I had any parasites. The results showed I had none. My intestines were clean after all those years of drinking ayahuasca." As parasites are common in the Amazon, it was noteworthy that Rafael Chanchari didn't have any.

I poured us both a glass of water. "And what can one learn by working with this plant?" I asked, shifting the conversation to ayahuasca's activity as a plant teacher.

"You can learn *icaros* [curing songs]. I have learned *icaros* that no human taught me. And I also learned to heal: I look after people when they fall ill and feel bad, and then they feel better. It's the same when they suffer from fear. Ayahuasca also teaches you to heal people with rheumatism and diabetes; when you drink ayahuasca, it tells you, 'this person is unwell and needs to take such-and-such plant.' So one learns gradually, and when a person shows up with symptoms of an illness that you have previously healed with a plant that ayahuasca told you about, then you know how to go about healing this person. That's experience. The person may wonder, 'How is it that just by looking at me, he knows which plant will heal me? He must be a sorcerer.' But no, it's just that we have had previous experience with other people. Through a voice we heard, ayahuasca told us which plant to use to heal the person. That's how one learns. What else can one learn from ayahuasca? To diagnose the illnesses that people have. When the person is ill, you drink ayahuasca, and then you see. In visions, doctors come, nurses come, men and women in long lines — this I have seen; they pass by and fill the house.

"These doctors are the mother of ayahuasca?"

"Yes, they are the mother of ayahuasca. They come in long lines, enter, pass next to me, carrying all their equipment, male and female doctors and nurses, and together they fill the house. And then you no longer see them. You only see them as they pass by, and then you no longer see them, but they are working all the while, healing, protecting, and defending those who are ill."

"Have you seen the mother of ayahuasca in your visions?"

"I have never seen the mother of ayahuasca, as such. I have seen entities in the form of a jaguar, or a bat, or small beings, or a hummingbird, but I have never seen a kind of person who shows up and says, 'I am the mother of ayahuasca,' neither as a man nor as a woman. But the entities I have seen can turn into men and women when they heal patients."

"When you saw a hummingbird, for example, how did you come to think that it was the mother of ayahuasca?"

"Because the mother of ayahuasca sometimes appears as a hummingbird, and other times in different forms. I once saw some lights that outlined an entire person, a whole human body surrounded by lights and walking toward those who were ill."

"Is the mother of ayahuasca masculine or feminine?"

"The word for ayahuasca in Shawi is *ka'pi*, which is a masculine word; but in Spanish, the word *ayahuasca* is feminine. In my experience, the mother of ayahuasca is of both sexes and can take the form of different beings: sometimes a woman, other times a man; sometimes a bird — a hummingbird, for example — other times an insect; sometimes a black boa snake, other times a yellow boa. Sometimes when there is healing to do, the mother of ayahuasca takes the form of a male doctor and a female doctor, or of military men and women when they have to defend the ill from sorcerer attacks. Ayahuasca has multiple mothers and souls, which can transform into different natural beings. If it is yellow, or sky, ayahuasca, it is associated with the yellow boa. And if it is black ayahuasca, it's with the black boa.

And sky ayahuasca has its own *icaro*. I have a song of the yellow boa that goes like this [he sings]: *u ru ru ri, u ru ru ri.* And when we sing this, the boa comes, shining and full of lights. That is its *uru*, which means 'to shine.'"

"So *icaros* allow you to call entities?"

"Yes, they are for calling. The yellow boa *icaro* is a song that ayahuasca taught me. During the first years when I was learning ayahuasca, I didn't know how to sing. One day I asked my uncle Lucas Pizuri Asipali, 'I don't hear *icaros* when I drink ayahuasca. How is it that you all sing?' He replied, 'Nephew, once you learn more, you will hear *icaros.*' I thought that *icaros* were simply learned from other people. But just as my uncle said, after drinking for years, I started to hear *icaros*, and that is how I learned to sing. I sing in my Shawi language. *Icaros* are not just for calling, but also for healing, for defending, and for enchanting people or calming sorcerers who look at you badly or who are angry. There are *icaros* for living well and for sending away the spirits who filled the house during the ceremony. This is necessary to do to protect the children, because these spirits can be strong in the presence of children. That's why it is our obligation to make them go back to where they came from, once we have used their services during the ceremony. It's a protocol we have for them. We invite them to our ceremonies when we take ayahuasca, and then we make them go back to their places of origin. We say 'mission accomplished' after putting an end to the ceremony."

"What illnesses can these entities heal?" I asked.

"They can cure people who think they have been bewitched. I have thought about this for some time, and in my opinion, a person who thinks they are bewitched will logically fall ill for some reason. It could be illness of the gallbladder, kidneys, lungs, muscles, or joints; or they get an ear or nose inflammation; or any other kind of disease. People who believe in sorcery already believe that they have been bewitched, and this belief is what exhausts them. And they often impose a risky diet on themselves — for example, they do not eat meat or fish with scales — and in doing this they deteriorate their body and take away its defenses, and things become increasingly complicated. So what does ayahuasca do? It comes and heals these people who think they have been bewitched. On the second day, as a *médico*, one might tell them, 'You are already cured — the spirit of ayahuasca has cured you.' And they will feel relieved, because they have freed themselves from what had trapped them psychically. As their spirits are freed, their bodies start to heal themselves. And you continue to give them ayahuasca to drink. I do not make them diet. I say, 'Eat, eat everything there is, but if it does you harm, stop eating immediately.' Because a sick person who stops eating will get worse.

"I had the case of a patient who had a fractured spine, according to the medical doctor. The young man had surely carried some heavy loads, and he fell ill. This was back home among Shawi people, in my community. He had been to several *médicos*, but they told him he was bewitched and was going to die. That's why he came to see me. And since he believes in sorcery, I gave him some ayahuasca to drink. I drank it too, and I diagnosed, and it was clear that there was a problem: the sorcery was in his mind, and it needed removing. How do you get rid of this? By saying 'There, I have taken it out of you. The ayahuasca has cured you.' And this freed him.

"Before coming to see me, he had gone to the hospital, and they had told him that he had to have an operation, but he didn't have any money and could not afford it. So what did we do? I told him, 'You have to rest. You are not going to carry anything; you are not going to work.' He was still thinking, 'I am going to die. I cannot get well. What other fate do I have? Surely, I will die.' Some days later, he was still staying with me, and I took ayahuasca and told him: 'You know what? You are thinking a lot about death. Now you have to change your way of being, your way of thinking.' To get him to believe me, I said, 'I am going to change your spirit. I am going to put another spirit in you, another spirit that thinks about life, healing, and living; this is what I am going to put in you.' And I sang to him, and looked after him well, and told him, 'Now, as of today, I don't believe that you will think about death. You have to think that you are going to heal.' And now he has grown fat, and he has stopped thinking about death."

Rafael Chanchari gave a clear description of how a *médico* could use ayahuasca to do healing work. But I had a nagging suspicion that the brew could also mislead people. So I asked, "Can ayahuasca deceive you?"

"Ayahuasca does not deceive," he replied. "People are the ones who deceive."

"Meaning that people deceive themselves?"

"Yes. Ayahuasca does not deceive you; ayahuasca tells the truth. How could ayahuasca deceive you? It looks at you and sees everything that you are and everything that you have, as well as when you will die. Because humans have to die at some point. Ayahuasca also makes you see that you will die."

"But I have seen people," I said, "mainly foreigners, who drink ayahuasca and then claim that ayahuasca told them to do such-and-such, and it turns out to be nonsense."

"Yes," he replied.

"So it seems to me that one needs to learn the difference between seeing things that are true and seeing things that are not. Does that seem right to you?" I asked.

"Yes," he replied. "Listen—"

"So," I said, interrupting him, "that means that ayahuasca misleads people, doesn't it?"

"It is not that ayahuasca lies, but rather that lies and truth exist in the world, and ayahuasca allows you to see this. Ayahuasca focuses on the great human values; on the environment of your personal life in the past, present, and future; on the greater aspects of life in a community, a nation, or the world. It does not focus on nonsense. And it allows you to see the negative impacts of human activities on the environment, through destruction and lack of care.

"There are rules to follow that have been tried and true since our ancestors' times, such as dieting for three days after drinking ayahuasca. The diet consists of avoiding hot foods and drinks, to go easy on the liver; and refraining from sexual relations, to avoid becoming weak.

"Ayahuasca teaches you values, such as respect. And it allows you to perfect yourself as a person. For example, it inculcates the nonconsumption of alcohol, drugs, and cigarettes. Perhaps the word *inculcate* is inexact, because ayahuasca does not inculcate; it simply makes it so that your body no longer needs to consume those things.

"Regarding your question, for my part I make a distinction between hallucinations and visions. In my experience, with ayahuasca, when you hear a message, it is true; and when you see a screen in front of you showing what is going on in the world, this is also true. But sometimes you have what seems like an intuition, and you think 'maybe that's how things are happening,' and this is not true."

"And how do you learn to tell the difference?"

"You need human values to be able to make the distinction. And this takes practice and experience, not just one or two days, but over a long period. Now that I have experience, the things I hear and see are true, but there are times when I have premonitions, and they are not true."

"So the problem is that one contributes to the process by making projections?"

"Yes, that's right. That's where the lie is: you have what feels like an intuition, you are imagining things, and then you affirm them, but they are not true. And this can even lead to crimes. Not so long ago here in Iquitos, two foreigners drank ayahuasca and then one killed the other, because he saw in his visions that his friend was sleeping with his wife. It is possible that this was a hallucination, or simply what he believed was going on, and he took it at face value, and affirmed it, and then unfortunate events happened."

"Seen from afar," I said, "ayahuasca can seem dangerous, because it can lead people into extreme situations, in this case all the way to death."

"Yes, it is dangerous. Among my Shawi people, people kill each other for such things. It is dangerous, because if a person does not know how to discern between the truth of ayahuasca and hallucinations, that is what happens."

"So how does one reduce the danger of ayahuasca?" I asked.

"It is difficult, because there are people who act, and they do not know how to control their emotions. I think the important thing is that each person has to learn to control their emotions. For example, when a man has the impression that his wife is cheating on him, this produces anger, and he may even attack her. This is what one has to know how to control. The key is control."

"One hears of *ayahuasqueros* who use their powers of enchantment to take advantage of women. Many practitioners seem to commit this kind of abuse. What do you think about this?"

"I think this is the reason why ayahuasca looks for healthy people. To be a *médico*, you have to be a healthy person, not just physically, but also mentally. Healthy mind in a healthy body. Because ayahuasca guides you toward good, not evil. But these are people who get carried away by emotions and instinct. They take advantage of others. This is wrong."

"So it depends a lot on the individual person?"

"It depends on the person, yes. For this reason, ayahuasca trains you, and teaches you, and talks to you about values and ethics. Once I was surprised when it talked to me about the ethics and morals of healing. It's true that a lot of practitioners take advantage of people, and when a patient consults them, they say, 'Ah, you have been bewitched. You are about to die.' One time, a woman from Lima came to my house and said, 'I was told that I am going to die in three days. That's why I am here.' 'And who told you this, ma'am?' I asked. 'A *médico*, and he wanted to charge me eight hundred soles [about US$215] to heal me.' 'Very well, ma'am, let's see.' I smoked some *mapacho* to calm down and concentrate on what was plaguing her. I saw that she had a problem in her mind, having to do with worry, anxiety, and other psychological troubles. So I told her, 'Ma'am, you are not bewitched. The other fellow did not cure you, because you are not bewitched; he only wanted to take your money. But when you leave my house, you will be in good health.' She was mentally blocked, decentered, and emotionally unbalanced to the point of thinking she was going to die. And all this was on a mental level. I told her, 'You are going to get well. You have arrived here today, tomorrow will be the second day, and on the third day you are *not* going to die — you are going to get well.' 'Oh, thank you!' she said. I blew tobacco smoke on her, as a stimulus for her to believe that she was on the mend. That's how *mapacho* works: when you are afraid because someone has told you you are going to die, you can free yourself with *mapacho*."

"And in your opinion, does the ayahuasca *médico* have to charge something?"

"In the old days, the service provided by a *médico* deserved recompense. Among Shawi people, when a *médico* healed someone, they would bring him an egg, or sometimes they brought him a chicken or some fish cooked in leaves, or they would give him a hand in his garden. 'We are going to help you, because you healed my wife, or my son, and so you deserve a recompense.' That's how it was in the old days. But now, everything is money. Gone are the eggs and fish wrapped in leaves. And many people take advantage of this to charge too much money. But when it comes to ayahuasca, payment can be symbolic. It can be an egg, or a canoe, or some work in the garden. It depends on the will of the person. In the old days, the traditional *médico* did not put a price on cures or treatments."

"Is the problem money itself, or the amount of money?"

"The problem is the amount. Because there are people who take advantage of others. Just look at the case of the woman from Lima: they told her that she was bewitched and that she would die in three days, and then they asked for eight hundred soles to heal her. But she said, 'No, I am going to Iquitos to look for someone who can tell me if this is true.' And she came."

"So what was the fair price in this case?"

"The woman who was going to die in three days, and who left three days later feeling freed, do you know how much she gave me? Two hundred soles. We talked, and I blew *mapacho* smoke to treat her fear, and this allowed her to free herself. And in thanks she gave me two hundred soles. Fair payment is determined by the will of the person who evaluates how much the *médico* truly deserves for the treatment."

CHAPTER 4

Discombobulating Therapeutic Cocktail

The Science of Ayahuasca

Banisteriopsis caapi,
vine, leaves, and flowers

Scientists have studied tobacco for longer and in greater depth than ayahuasca. As of the sixteenth century, tobacco fascinated observers around the world,[1] whereas ayahuasca remained an obscure Amazonian hallucinogen until the second part of the twentieth century. The science of ayahuasca is just getting started.

Consider the question of botanical varieties. Scientists list seventy-six different *Nicotiana* species, with widely varying alkaloid contents, including several plants that do not produce nicotine.[2] But the botanical identity of the ayahuasca vine is another story. Amazonian people have long recognized different kinds of ayahuasca, which are "easy to distinguish ... by their color and shape," as Rafael Chanchari put it.[3] Some have big knots on their stems, while others do not; and the color of the bark and the inner wood varies. But ethnobotanists have insisted that only one species of ayahuasca exists, *Banisteriopsis caapi*. In the 1970s and 1980s, Richard Evans Schultes, the foremost ethnobotanist of the twentieth century, called the indigenous perspective on ayahuasca "an avenue for future research" and "an enigma."[4] But the question has remained largely unexplored. In 2018, an interdisciplinary group of researchers finally called for a review of the botanical classification of the ayahuasca vine based on the visible and widely recognized differences between vines.[5]

Why scientists have taken so long to look into the "enigma" of ayahuasca varieties is itself an enigma. Genetic studies of the different plants conducted in dialogue with Amazonian experts seem like a place to start.[6]

THE TROUBLE WITH AYAHUASCA'S
ACTIVE PRINCIPLE

There has also been some confusion in the scientific identification of ayahuasca's "active principle." In the 1970s, anthropologists and chemists examined the molecular contents of ayahuasca brews to find that they often, but not always, contained DMT, a powerful hallucinogen that normally is orally inactive because of a stomach enzyme that dissolves it; as the brew also contains harmala alkaloids that block this very stomach enzyme, the researchers formulated a hypothesis: the ayahuasca brew is actually a form of orally active DMT. This hypothesis became the accepted scientific orthodoxy in the 1980s and has stayed in place since then. No matter if the DMT found in ayahuasca brews comes from admixture plants, rather than from the aya-huasca vine itself. No matter if the ayahuasca vine's harmala alkaloids — harmine, harmaline, and tetrahydroharmine — are also psychoactive to a certain extent. And no matter if the DMT-centered explanation implies that Amazonian people are mistaken to consider the ayahuasca vine as the central compo-nent of the brew that bears its name.[7]

An additional problem with the DMT-centered explanation is that ayahuasca made from vine alone does indeed induce visions, albeit less colorful and spectacular ones than DMT-containing brews. In the words of ethnobotanist Wade Davis: "Taken alone, an infusion of the plant induces subtle visions, blues and pur-ples, slow undulating waves of color."[8]

In some parts of the Amazon, people prepare brews or in-fusions made from pure ayahuasca vines, without any additives, either by boiling pieces of vine for several hours or by macerat-ing mashed vines in cold water. In 1874, botanist Richard Spruce related the preparation of a cold-water extract of *Banisteriopsis caapi* in the Vaupés region of Colombia, writing, "The lower part of the stem is the part used. A quantity of this is beaten in a mortar, with water…. When sufficiently triturated, it is passed through a sieve, which separates the woody fiber, and to the resi-due enough water is added to render it drinkable. Thus prepared, its color is brownish-green, and its taste is bitter and disagree-able." Almost one hundred years later, anthropologist Gerardo Reichel-Dolmatoff described the same method of preparation in the same area of Colombia: "Several pieces of the fresh *Banis-teriopsis* vine, about the thickness of a finger, are mashed in a wooden trough, with cold water added later. The liquid is passed through a sieve to remove fibrous material and small pieces of bark and is then collected in a decorated ceramic vessel made especially for this purpose." Reichel-Dolmatoff drank six cups of this infusion and reported seeing visions of peacock tails, fireworks, Oriental and Tibetan tapestries, undulating colors in motion, and microphotographs of plants, among many other things — leaving little doubt that vine-only extracts have visionary properties.[9]

More recently, researchers doing fieldwork among Amazonian people have reported the effects and implications of drinking vine-only ayahuasca. Linguist Gayle Highpine writes on the basis of her fieldwork among Napo Runa people in Ecuador:

> Ayahuasca vine is not visionary in the same way as DMT. Visions from vine-only brews are shadowy, monochromatic, like silhouettes, or curling smoke, or clouds moving across the night sky. It is because their visions are usually monochromatic that vines are classified by the color of vision they produce: white, black, blue, red (in my experience, dark maroon). Snakes, the most common vision on ayahuasca, are considered the manifest spirit of the vine. Vine visions can be hard to see; in fact, the "visions" may not be visual at all, but auditory or somatic or intuitive. But the vine carries the *content* of the message, the teaching, and the insight. The leaf helps illuminate the content, but the teachings are credited to the vine.... The vine is The Teacher, The Healer, The Guide. The purpose

of drinking ayahuasca is to receive the message the
vine imparts. This is why it is the vine, not the leaf,
that is classified by the type of vision it gives.[10]

By "leaf," Highpine is referring to the DMT-containing leaves of the admixture plants, which are added to the pounded ayahuasca vines during the brew's preparation.

In an article entitled "Drinking Ayahuasca without DMT Is Powerful and Traditional," chemist Matteo Politi describes drinking vine-only ayahuasca as a powerful experience that made him incapable of standing up or walking and induced purging, visions, and deep states of mindfulness. This lack of motor coordination dovetails with reports by people who have ingested large doses of harmaline — a substance that can also induce abundant, vivid, and bright-colored imagery in people with closed eyes. This suggests that harmaline may play an important role in the effects of vine-only ayahuasca.[11]

The same can be said of tetrahydroharmine; according to chemist Jace C. Callaway, who analyzed thirty-five samples of *Banisteriopsis caapi* and found significant correlations between alkaloid content and the subjective effects of the ayahuasca brews they produced: "In particular, experienced drinkers seem to prefer those teas where tetrahydroharmine concentrations were high, compared to harmine and harmaline. They explained that such teas delivered more 'force' to the experience."[12]

Harmine also has detectable psychoactive effects. And the interactions and synergies of the vine's numerous alkaloids have yet to be studied and may contribute to its visionary properties. Scientists call this the "entourage" effect, whereby the different alkaloids present in the vine "cooperate" to produce a final result more effective than the different compounds in their pure form and separately.[13]

In recent years, scientists have come to understand that the substances contained in the ayahuasca vine have a broad spectrum of health-enhancing properties. All three harmala alkaloids induce the formation of new neurons; harmine, in particular, also has anti-inflammatory, analgesic, antimicrobial, antioxidative, antiaddictive, antidepressive, and possibly anti-Parkinson's and antitumor properties.[14]

Ethnobotanist Dale Millard comments:

> It seems that there has indeed been a bias in the Western understanding of ayahuasca towards visionary aspects and experiential phenomena. Although these are considered paramount to the experience and research into the potential for ayahuasca in treating psychiatric and psychological problems is gaining momentum, little is known to date about the application of this medicine in treating diseases of the body. It is only through anecdotal information that we know that Amazonian practitioners use ayahuasca for a wide variety of physiological diseases and complaints. Harmine already demonstrated a remarkably broad spectrum of activity, which supports the hypothesis that, if taken at regular intervals in nontoxic dosages, as is the case in the vast majority of ayahuasca drinkers, it may well have wide-reaching and positive health-enhancing properties. The

evidence presented thus far, in particular concerning diseases for which conventional medicine is
currently challenged, demonstrates the usefulness
of this compound, and specifically of ayahuasca,
as a potential medicine not only in the treatment
of psychiatric and psychosomatic problems but in
a wide variety of human physiological patholo-
gies. The seemingly remarkable ability of harmine
to interfere with crucial metabolic processes in
such a wide range of pathological organisms and
cancerous cells, but still promote the healthy out-
growth of neural networks, bone and joint tissues
and pancreatic β cells, is of great interest and im-
portance, especially as these tissues normally de-
generate in all of us with age.[15]

Current research on the health-enhancing properties of the
substances contained in the ayahuasca vine certainly agrees with
the Amazonian view that the vine itself is the brew's main constituent.[16]

The tendency of contemporary scientists to attribute the
effects of ayahuasca exclusively to the DMT it sometimes contains needs reconsidering. For some Amazonian experts, the
DMT-containing admixture plants merely serve to brighten and
clarify the visions, which makes it easier for the beginner — but
an experienced *ayahuasquero* learns to see visions even in low
light. From this perspective, the spectacular colored visions produced by DMT are mere distractions or "side effects."[17]

As Rafael Chanchari says, drinking vine-only ayahuasca is
"good for the health; it strengthens you and gives you visions."

AYAHUASCA AS A COMPLEX COCKTAIL

Scientists like to standardize the substances they study, because the scientific method requires repeated tests in different times and places, with no variation in the object of study.[18] But there is no "standard" ayahuasca. Any given mixture contains the ayahuasca vine, but beyond this basis, the other contents depend entirely on the person preparing the brew. Ethnobotanist Jonathan Ott lists ninety-seven Amazonian plant species as confirmed ayahuasca additives, including tobacco, *toé*, coca, and two DMT-containing species including *Psychotria viridis* (chacruna). This means that any given brew may, or may not, contain nicotine, scopolamine, cocaine, or DMT, all of which are potent psychoactive substances in their own right. Ott suggests thinking of ayahuasca as "an all-purpose pharmacological vehicle." This being the case, providing a precise molecular definition of ayahuasca is impossible.[19]

As historian Constantino Manuel Torres puts it: "An investigation into the origins of ayahuasca reveals numerous beverages distributed throughout South America, each distinct, varying according to plant availability, cultural predilections for ingestion, and ritual requirements. No fixed recipe exists, and the composition of the potion varies."[20]

In 2020, researcher Helle Kaasik and her colleagues analyzed the chemical composition of 102 samples of ayahuasca from different locations and found on average 54 percent more DMT in brews from neo-shamanic facilitators than in those from indigenous Amazonian shamans. For Kaasik, these DMT-heavy brews "emphasize tripping over healing."[21]

Even a pure vine extract, containing no additive whatsoever, is a complex cocktail containing numerous bioactive compounds besides the harmala alkaloids, which may contribute to its effects.[22]

One thing is certain: before drinking ayahuasca, people gain from knowing about the liquid's true contents. There have been cases in Europe of so-called ayahuasca containing no Amazonian plants at all, with pharmaceutical antidepressants added to the mixture.[23]

As Rafael Chanchari says, it is important to ask the person who administers the brew what it contains; and the practitioner needs to be honest.

AYAHUASCA'S EFFECTS ON THE BRAIN AND BODY

Scientists who study ayahuasca often state that they do not fully grasp how ayahuasca works in the brain and the body.[24] However, neuroscientists have recently made spectacular progress in understanding the workings of other hallucinogens like psilocybin and LSD, by using brain imaging technology. In brief, the molecules of these substances get into the brain and bind to serotonin receptors on precise neurons, which usually play a key role in organizing the brain's overall activities. By exciting these neurons and disrupting their normal activity, these hallucinogenic molecules decrease brain activity in important centers for information integration and routing in the brain. This allows distinct networks of neurons to communicate more easily with one another, and the brain seems to operate with greater flexibility and interconnectedness under hallucinogens.[25]

In the case of ayahuasca, brain imaging studies are still small in number. Those that exist all involve DMT-containing ayahuasca and yield results similar to those produced by psilocybin and LSD studies, implicating the same serotonin receptors and a similar disruption of brain activity. Yet DMT-containing ayahuasca also has its differences with the other hallucinogens; in particular, it stimulates the visual cortex just as much as seeing natural images with open eyes; and it stimulates an area in the frontal cortex involved with intentional prospective imagination, which is active when people find solutions to problems. So brain imagery confirms, at least in a preliminary fashion, that drinking DMT-containing ayahuasca allows one to see vivid images with closed eyes, and to find solutions.[26]

Unfortunately, neuroscientific research has yet to study the impact on the human brain of vine-only ayahuasca.

Besides neuroscience, recent scientific research has found that the ritual and clinical use of ayahuasca has therapeutic potential for treating and managing a series of diseases and ailments, including depression, post-traumatic stress disorder, anxiety, and addiction.[27]

When scientists run clinical trials on ayahuasca, they invariably use the DMT-containing brews, which they tend to present as the "typical" or "standard" version.[28]

Clinical trials have shown this kind of ayahuasca to be relatively safe, with no evidence of physiological toxicity in long-term users. It does not appear to have a negative impact on the body.[29]

Of course, this says nothing about the ayahuasca that people may run into outside the laboratory, and which could contain nicotine, or scopolamine, and turn out to be toxic or even lethal.

Over the years, there have been several reports of deaths associated with the consumption of ayahuasca, but in all cases, it would seem that other substances were to blame. No forensic analysis was made in any of the cases. And death has never been reported in a clinical trial of ayahuasca.[30]

Ayahuasca itself, understood as the scientifically sanctioned version of the brew containing a strict combination of the ayahuasca vine and the DMT-containing leaves of the *Psychotria viridis* (chacruna) bush, seems relatively innocuous physically. The lethal dose for this kind of ayahuasca is estimated at twenty times the usual effective dose. This corresponds roughly to about two liters of ayahuasca, an improbable amount to imbibe; the brew often tastes foul and provokes vomiting, so it seems highly unlikely that anybody could drink such a quantity and manage to keep it down long enough for death to ensue. In comparison, alcohol can be fatal at ten times its effective dose, indicating that "oral DMT in ayahuasca has acceptable toxicity in humans"[31] and that, based on research, it is less lethal than alcohol.

In fact, recent research suggests that reasonable doses of DMT may play a positive role in the human body, most notably in tissue protection, neuron regeneration, and immune system enhancement.[32]

Like other classical hallucinogens, ayahuasca is not considered addictive. On the contrary, there is now considerable evidence that it acts as an antiaddictive, helping people move away from their dependency on substances like alcohol, opiates, and cocaine. There are several possible explanations for this. One is that the harmine and harmaline contained in the brew stimulate the release of dopamine in the brain's "reward center," which reduces craving and the desire for repeated self-administration; and simultaneously, the brew's DMT stimulates serotonin receptors in a way that inhibits the release of dopamine in the same center. So ayahuasca seems to both raise and lower dopamine levels in key parts of the brain, which results in a balancing, or normalizing, effect on dopamine levels.[33]

Another possible explanation for ayahuasca's antiaddictive properties is its capacity to promote the growth of new neurons. Besides DMT's possible activity in the regeneration of neurons, harmine, harmaline, and tetrahydroharmine have all been shown to do this on living cells in the laboratory. It could be that ayahuasca helps "rewire" neural connections within the dopamine reward center that have been overtaken by addictive behaviors, by promoting the formation of new neural networks; and this may decrease addictive behaviors.[34]

In addition, preliminary research indicates that ayahuasca enhances cognition and learning. Laboratory studies have shown that harmine improves learning and memory in rodents. And one recent study demonstrated long-term improvements in cognitive thinking style in healthy ayahuasca users.[35]

Research also suggests that ayahuasca acts as an antidepressant. Preliminary studies indicate that a single dose of ayahuasca produces significant reduction in depressive symptoms for at least twenty-one days in patients with recurrent depression. One recent study showed that a single dose of ayahuasca produces significant clinical improvements in 80 percent of patients, with the effect lasting six months. The scientists involved in this research suggest that ayahuasca's antidepressive effects may be due to its capacity to increase blood flow in brain areas related to depressive symptoms.[36]

This research echoes Rafael Chanchari's treatment of the young man with the fractured spine: as a *médico*, he gave him a single dose of ayahuasca in order to change his depressed mindset, with conclusive results.

CONTRAINDICATIONS, ADVERSE EFFECTS, AND THE DARK SIDE OF AYAHUASCA

Scientists have begun to recognize the therapeutic potential of ayahuasca, and this comes with a list of contraindications. Ayahuasca is not recommended for people who suffer from psychosis, schizophrenia, bipolar disorder, or cardiovascular disease or who use pharmaceutical drugs such as antidepressants, anti-anxiety agents, hypertension drugs, amphetamines, sedatives, or sleeping pills. Nor is it recommended for pregnant women.[37]

Beyond these contraindications, it sometimes happens that healthy individuals who have prepared themselves appropriately, and who drink well-administered ayahuasca, nonetheless end up feeling deeply discombobulated by the experience. Ayahuasca can have a distressing and destructuring effect on people. This rare phenomenon, which scientists call a "transitory psychotic crisis," remains understudied and requires further investigation.[38]

The fact is that consuming ayahuasca is necessarily a risky proposition. Inasmuch as the brew acts as a "psychedelic" —

meaning "psyche-revealing" — you take a risk with your own psyche when you drink it. You never know what this potent hallucinogen will reveal about yourself until you have swallowed it; but then it's too late to turn back.

Anthropologist Luis Eduardo Luna pinpoints part of the problem:

> The greatest dangers of ayahuasca do not concern potential adverse physiological problems, which are few and can be avoided through proper information, nor even psychological problems, which in most cases can be controlled through proper set and setting (though, of course anyone with serious psychotic issues should abstain from ayahuasca). The real problem has to do with ego inflation, to which no one is impervious. This may take the form of messianic delusions and abuse of various kinds, such as taking advantage of the vulnerable situation in which inexperienced people find themselves, either due to their fear, their ingenuousness or their gratitude towards the person who facilitated their experiences with ayahuasca.[39]

Taking advantage of people who have consumed ayahuasca has unfortunately become a widespread phenomenon, in particular when it comes to male ayahuasca practitioners sexually abusing and assaulting women. Numerous reports to this effect have surfaced in recent years.[40]

Drinking ayahuasca makes people suggestible and takes

down their defenses. This is part of the brew's transformational potential — but it also puts users in a vulnerable mindset. Unscrupulous practitioners take advantage of this. As psychologist Rachel Harris points out, all the reports and complaints to date of rape and sexual abuse concern male ayahuasca practitioners abusing females.[41]

Rafael Chanchari suggests that people who work with ayahuasca need to grasp the difference between ayahuasca visions and their own projections, and to learn self-control. This requires long and difficult training, as well as following tried-and-true prescriptions, such as avoiding certain foods and refraining from sexual relations before and after drinking the brew.

Scientists who study the therapeutic potential of ayahuasca gain from taking the brew's dark side into consideration, if they are to reach a full understanding.

AYAHUASCA CALLS FOR A NEW KIND OF RESEARCH

For Amazonian people, an important part of ayahuasca's efficacy lies in its power as a purgative.[42] That's why they call it *la purga*. As Rafael Chanchari says, the brew cleans the stomach and intestines and gets rid of intestinal parasites. And scientific studies confirm that the harmala alkaloids contained in the ayahuasca vine have antiparasitic properties.[43]

But when it comes to purging proper, the scientists who study ayahuasca in laboratories and clinics most often list vomiting as an "adverse effect." Some even propose to administer encapsulated freeze-dried ayahuasca to their research subjects to reduce vomiting.[44] For scientists to truly understand *la purga*, they may have to recognize that using the "psychedelic" ayahuasca involves first and foremost an intensely corporeal experience.

One recent ethnographic study of Western ayahuasca users confirmed the therapeutic virtues of ayahuasca purging. Participants reported expulsing not just toxic substances that had accumulated in their bodies but also "psychic garbage" and past traumatic experiences.[45]

Beyond the basic question of purging, Amazonian experts affirm that *icaros* (curative songs or chants) have healing power, and refraining from certain foods and behaviors can fine-tune a person's capacity to learn from ayahuasca. However, it seems unlikely that scientific protocols will include *icaros* or *dietas* (preparatory diets) anytime soon.[46]

A true science of ayahuasca calls for a new kind of research — one that opens up to another way of knowing, without the need to either "believe in it" or "not believe in it." In the words of anthropologist Eduardo Viveiros de Castro: "For a start, taking native thought seriously is to refuse to neutralize it." This means refusing to explain it or rationalize it, and instead drawing out its consequences and verifying the effects it can produce on one's own thinking. Belief has nothing to do with this process, as Viveiros de Castro points out, and couching indigenous thought in terms of belief or disbelief means placing it on the grounds of theology; whereas singing certain melodies to impact people who have drunk ayahuasca, or preparing their bodies and minds before and after the experience, appears to have more to do with the practicalities of being in the world.[47]

To engage in a true dialogue with Amazonian experts, scientists will need to become aware of their own presuppositions — and this is where ayahuasca may come in, because the brew is known to help people do just that.[48]

MORE FRICTIONS BETWEEN WESTERN AND INDIGENOUS VIEWS

Amazonian experts view ayahuasca as a being, similar to a human being. Working with this plant teacher means developing a relationship based on respect.

Scientists tend to have difficulty with the "animistic"[49] concept of plant teachers — even though research shows that ayahuasca enhances cognition and learning and lights up areas in the brain associated with seeing images and finding solutions.

As previously stated, one's position on such matters depends on one's understanding of reality. People are free to think whatever they wish, including that the "mother" of ayahuasca is no more than the result of the impact of the brew's alkaloids on human neurons and that the concept is an unnecessary personification. However, it is interesting to note a trend to the contrary in this case: a growing number of Western ayahuasca users tend to personify and feminize the plant and brew by referring to an entity they call "Grandmother Ayahuasca."[50]

This diverges with the Amazonian view, which approaches the gender of ayahuasca with greater ambiguity.[51] As Rafael Chanchari says, the "mother" or "owner" of ayahuasca can take the form of a hummingbird, a snake, a jaguar, a bat, a long line of female and male doctors and nurses, an army of male and female soldiers, and many other beings besides.

Ayahuasca has no fixed recipe and no fixed persona.

Though considerably less toxic than tobacco, ayahuasca remains a *pharmakon*, both a medicine and a poison. It can heal, teach, purge, and discombobulate, all in one.

As Rafael Chanchari says, all teacher plants, including tobacco and ayahuasca, have "two souls." They are ambiguous by nature, and they can get those who work with them into trouble.

In this little book, we combine indigenous knowledge and science because they provide a rich complement to each other, and because their juxtaposition makes a wide range of information available to those who may be interested.

We do not encourage people to use tobacco or ayahuasca, but to understand that approaching these powerful plants requires prudence, respect, and knowledge.

CONCLUSION

This short book lays out two ways of considering psycho-active plants. Integrating these two approaches into a co-herent and holistic understanding is a complex undertaking. I do not wish to tell readers how to proceed on this count because it is important to allow people to reach their own conclusions according to their views of the world. But I can give a testimony about how I deal with the question on a personal basis.

As previously stated, I was educated in rationalism and ma-terialism. To this day, if I want to understand something — a virus, a plant, a vaccine — I look into what science says about it. I want to know about the molecules I take into my body, and if possible, what they do once they're inside.

And because I take molecules seriously, I know that there

are many things science does not understand. Scientists may have determined that nicotine plays an important part in tobacco's activity, but they have no clear idea about what goes on in the body, brain, and mind of a tobacco shaman who is "turning into a jaguar."

Having had the privilege of spending time with Amazonian people, I know they have deep knowledge about plants, bodies, and minds that they express in personalized terms, rather than in molecular ones. Time and again I have found that taking their views seriously leads to verifiable and useful knowledge. Now I consider indigenous Amazonian knowledge as a coherent way of knowing that can be used in parallel to science.

I compare using these two systems of knowledge to speaking two languages. As a bilingual person, I know that English allows one to say things that French does not, and vice versa. For example, there is no real French equivalent for the word *pattern*; the dictionary proposes static words meaning "design," "sketch," or "model" or else words meaning "habit" or "tendency" — but nothing that renders the evolving and time-rich qualities of the original concept. Likewise, the French word *démarche* gets translated as "walk," "gait," or "approach," but English has no concept of a full-blown *démarche*, which verges on "intellectual reasoning" or "philosophy" while remaining personal and specific. So thinking the world in English or in French is not the same, even for someone fluent in both languages. Of course, translation from one to the other is always possible. But exact word-for-word translations tend to sound strange, and translators face the dilemma of making less-faithful choices to convey the rhythm or emotion of the original — meaning that translation can border on betrayal. And some things simply do not translate at all. None of this means that one language is better than the other, just that speaking both well, and going back and forth between the two, takes constant practice. And starting young also helps.

The same is true when it comes to combining science and indigenous knowledge. Allow me to give an example. If I am asked to address the subject of the true nature of plants, I will start by asking myself, "How would Amazonians look at this? And how would scientists look at it?" Since 1990 or so, the scientific view of plants has moved away from a strictly materialist and mindless perspective, and scientists now recognize that plants perceive, communicate, decide, learn, and remember. They may not be ready to personify plants just yet, but they have moved closer to the indigenous view of plants as intelligent entities. So do plants have personalities? For instance, does tobacco really have a "mother"? Many years ago, I had great difficulty taking the notion of "the mother of tobacco" seriously. But I no longer see a problem in considering that the plant has something like a powerful personality. In my experience, consuming tobacco was like meeting a fiery person. As a young anthropologist, I found that a single dose of strong tobacco impacted my personality: it made me feel warm, powerful, predatory, and wise — and in such a deep way that I can summon those feelings decades later and tap into them. I do not ask anybody to believe that tobacco *really* has a personality. Nor am I sure that I believe it really does either. In fact, I am not that interested in belief. But I do think that considering tobacco *as if* it has a personality is interesting, and probably not that far off the mark.

Scientists, meanwhile, refuse to personify, and insist on

objectifying, because such is their method. So they refuse to consider the "personality" of tobacco, and I regret this imposed limit, even though I understand it. But beyond that, I pay attention to what scientists are willing to say on the matter. And the scientific view is that the plant's nicotine molecules have all kinds of impacts on our heartbeat and hormones; adrenaline, dopamine, endorphins, testosterone, estrogen — all these substances flood our system when we consume tobacco. And I have little doubt that there is a connection between this and my having felt warm, powerful, predatory, and wise when I swallowed the paste of the old tobacco shaman all those years ago.

I do not mean that the scientific reading based on molecules and hormones *explains* my "jaguar transformation" experience. But I think the nicotine and the hormones contributed to it. Both views can be true at the same time: a scientist will talk about hormone levels, a shaman will talk about jaguar transformation — both are referring to the same event, but in two different languages. Neither is "more right" than the other.

Regarding the demise of Carlos Perez Shuma's father-in-law, who transformed into a jaguar by taking a strong dose of tobacco juice and then died because his heart burned as sweat poured off him: it is interesting to note that nicotine overdose can cause heart attacks, of which profuse sweating is the foremost symptom. Once again, I am not claiming to explain in rational terms a story that I found wildly irrational at the time of hearing it. Rather, I think a nicotine-induced heart attack is a possibility that easily complements the original story — but it is also unprovable, because the events happened too long ago.

By opening up to the validity of indigenous knowledge as a

second way of knowing and as a complement to science, I feel better equipped to try to make sense of the world. I have more concepts, more angles, and more possible scenarios.

I talked this over with Rafael Chanchari, and he wholeheartedly agrees. As a bilingual person, he finds himself going back and forth on a daily basis between Shawi and Spanish, and between indigenous knowledge and science. He says he feels as if he has two drawers in his mind, one for each language, and they can communicate with each other. In his view, all bilingual people have this ability to go back and forth. He describes it as a skill that one develops over time, like juggling.

I think the key to integrating two different ways of knowing is to go back and forth between the two often enough and over a long period of time. Practice makes perfect.

And though this takes work and dedication, I tell myself that bilinguals have more fun.

APPENDIX

Vape, Snuff, *Rapé*, and Snus

An estimated 50 million people worldwide use electronic cigarettes, or "vape," and 300 million people use smokeless tobacco such as snuff, *rapé* (pronounced "ha-PAY") and snus (pronounced "snoose"). Users of these products seem to have a significantly lower overall mortality rate compared to cigarette smokers.[1] But this does not mean that they are harmless. For readers who may be interested, this appendix provides an overview of the health risks they present.

VAPE

Electronic cigarettes, or e-cigarettes, are a recent phenomenon, and their effects on human health remain largely unstudied.

There are thousands of e-juice flavors available to consumers, but few studies to date have examined the effects of exposure to flavorings. E-cigarette liquids have undergone minimal regulation, and their potential adverse effects are not well understood.[2]

E-cigarettes emit aerosol, rather than vapor. *Vapor* is the gaseous state of a substance that is normally solid or liquid, for example, water vapor; whereas aerosol is a liquid or a solid composed of finely divided particles suspended in a gaseous medium, for example, flea powder spray. In fact, "vaping" is misnamed.[3]

In 2016, an initial study showed that over 90 percent of commercially available e-cigarettes contain flavoring agents, chiefly diacetyl and 2,3-pentanedione. These substances — which give a creamy taste and contribute to flavors such as butter, caramel, piña colada, and strawberry — are considered safe in foods. But when they are heated to the point of aerosolization, they can irreversibly obstruct the lungs' smallest airways. This condition first appeared in the early 2000s in workers who had inhaled artificial butter flavor in microwave popcorn–processing facilities; initially dubbed "popcorn lung," it is now called "flavorings-related lung disease," or obliterative bronchiolitis.[4]

It is difficult to understand why e-cigarettes continue to include substances linked to such a respiratory disease. In 2019, public health specialist Joseph Allen, who conducted the initial research into the toxic components of e-cigarette flavors, commented: "E-cigarette users are heating and inhaling flavoring chemicals that were never tested for inhalation safety. Although some e-cigarette manufacturers are stating that they do not use diacetyl or 2,3-pentanedione, it begs an important question — what chemicals, then, are they using for flavoring? Further, workers receive warnings about the dangers of inhaling flavoring chemicals. Why aren't e-cigarette users receiving the same warnings?"[5]

Another problematic aspect of e-cigarettes involves the devices themselves. Some e-cigarettes allow users to turn up the heat generated by the electric coil to increase aerosol production and nicotine delivery, and this can radically alter the chemical composition of the aerosols they produce. In most cases, more than 90 percent of e-cigarette liquid is made up of glycerine and propylene glycol, which show no evidence of toxicity as food additives. Glycerine is an oily liquid with a warm, sweet taste, and propylene glycol is colorless and tasteless, but when they are combusted at high temperatures, they decompose to form the carcinogens formaldehyde and acetaldehyde. Research shows that turning up the voltage of e-cigarettes from 3.2 V to 4.8 V results in an increase of up to two hundred times in the levels of these carcinogenic substances, putting them in the range of levels reported in cigarette smoke.[6] In one recent study, researchers tested commercially available e-cigarette products and found that they all generated formaldehyde and acetaldehyde — in most cases at levels well below those observed in industrial tobacco cigarettes, but in some cases above those levels. They attributed the higher levels to devices with heater coils that exceeded 350°C during puffing. As temperatures rose above this threshold, formaldehyde and acetaldehyde levels increased steeply.[7] This indicates that the toxicity of e-cigarettes depends not only on their contents, but on how people use them.

Recent studies have also found that e-cigarette aerosols

contain metals, such as lead, nickel, cadmium, and chromium. One possible explanation for this is that metals in the heater coil leach during the heating process. In 2018, researchers Pablo Olmedo and colleagues sampled fifty-six e-cigarette devices from daily users and found significant increases in toxic metal concentrations once e-liquids had been aerosolized: lead and zinc each increased by more than 2,000 percent, and chromium, nickel, and tin by more than 600 percent each. The concentration of metals found in the aerosols "exceeded current health-based limits in close to 50% or more of the samples for chromium, manganese, nickel, and lead." They concluded, "These findings support the hypothesis that metals are transferred from the device (most likely the coil) to the e-liquid and from the e-liquid to the aerosol that is inhaled by the user."[8]

When metals are inhaled, rather than ingested, they stay in the body at significantly higher levels. Some metals, like zinc, manganese, copper, chromium, and nickel, are essential elements that are vital to human health in trace amounts — but they tend to become toxic when inhaled. Chromium and nickel have been associated with lung cancer. And lead is toxic no matter which way you absorb it.[9]

One recent study showed that minute particles of copper in e-cigarette aerosols damage lung cells, and in particular their DNA, which the particles break. Researchers found that an aerosol exposure lasting five minutes made no difference to the integrity of lung cell DNA, but exposure sessions longer than ten minutes resulted in significant damage.[10] This suggests that greater frequency and duration of e-cigarette use increase its toxicity.

And most e-cigarettes contain nicotine,[11] which is highly

addictive and has considerable impacts on human physiology and health.

The science of "vaping" is still in its infancy, and much research remains to be conducted. There may already be a new generation of e-cigarettes that are safer than others, with heating coils that neither leach metal nor heat beyond the critical threshold of 350°C. Some brands may already provide e-liquids devoid of harmful flavoring chemicals. But in the current unregulated state of the market, it is hard to be sure of much.

Consumers would certainly gain from knowing about the contents of the e-liquids they aerosolize and inhale, and from paying attention to the quality of the device they use and to the temperature at which they set it.

Given that e-cigarettes are a recent phenomenon, their impacts on human health are only just becoming apparent. Some consumers are beginning to present "vaping-associated pulmonary injury." The deteriorating lungs of frequent users become chronically inflamed, which can cause a series of problems, including increased vulnerability to respiratory diseases like Covid-19.[12]

SNUFF

Unlike e-cigarettes, snuff has a long history of human usage, and does not seem to affect the lungs. It is not to be confused with chewing tobacco, which is made of loose leaves, braided leaves (called a twist), or compressed leaves (called a plug). Commercially available snuff comes in the form of a dark and fine powder made from fermented and fire-cured tobacco, which users either inhale through the nose or suck between the cheek and gum.

When sucked, snuff is also called "dip." Snuff contains none of the tar or toxic gases produced by burning cigarettes nor any of the harmful substances specific to e-cigarette aerosols. But it comes with risks of its own.

Snuffing delivers nicotine to the blood almost as efficiently as smoking and vaping, because the linings of the mouth and nose easily and quickly absorb it.[13] This means that snuff is as addictive as cigarettes and e-cigarettes.

Like most forms of commercial tobacco — including pipe, cigar, shisha, and chewing tobacco — snuff contains powerful carcinogens called nitrosamines. These substances form during the curing and processing of tobacco, as bacteria produce nitrite that degrades the plant's alkaloids. Green tobacco leaves contain virtually no nitrosamines. The presence of these toxic substances in tobacco products varies greatly, depending on tobacco variety, agricultural practices such as fertilization, and curing methods. Storing conditions also make a difference, as the longer tobacco products stay on the shelf at room temperature, the higher their nitrosamine levels tend to be. One thing is certain: consuming any tobacco with high levels of nitrosamines is dangerous, because these substances have a remarkable ability to induce tumors of the oral cavity, esophagus, and nasal mucosa.[14]

Research on snuff use confirms this. Snuffing raises the risk of cancer of the nose, sinus, mouth, throat, cheek, gums, lips, tongue, esophagus, and pancreas. It also raises the risk of heart attack, heart disease, high blood pressure, stroke, and type 2 diabetes — and the more one snuffs, the higher the risks. When used during pregnancy, snuff increases the risk of early delivery and stillbirth.[15]

SNUS

Like snuff, Nordic snus is a powdered form of tobacco, but its impacts on human health seem less severe. Originally produced in Sweden, it contains tobacco that is air-dried and steam-pasteurized, rather than fermented and fire-cured. This limits the growth of bacteria that facilitate the formation of nitrosamines. Some Swedish brands all but eliminate the nitrosamine problem by excluding bacteria from the production process; they also choose tobacco plants fertilized with low levels of nitrogen, which further limits the development of nitrosamines. And Nordic snus products are generally kept refrigerated at sale points, which may also hinder the growth of bacteria and the generation of nitrosamines.[16]

For years, studies of the adverse health effects of Nordic snus were inconclusive — in stark contrast to other tobacco products. But Swedish scientists recently demonstrated that Nordic snus users do run a higher risk of developing type 2 diabetes — with heavy users presenting a risk similar to that of cigarette smokers. Nicotine is known to increase insulin resistance and therefore the risk of type 2 diabetes. Given that consumption of Nordic snus is not conclusively linked to cardiovascular disease or cancer, Sofia Carlsson and colleagues, who conducted this research, commented: "the diabetes-promoting effect of cigarettes and snus is hence likely to be mediated by nicotine, whereas the tobacco-related risks of cardiovascular disease and cancer may be due to other components of tobacco smoke."[17]

Nordic snus seems to present less risk to human health than most other tobacco products. Studies indicate that its users have a low incidence of tobacco-related mortality.[18] But Nordic snus remains banned in the European Union, and only a handful of countries allow its distribution, including Sweden, Norway, South Africa, and the United States. Perhaps this is because Nordic snus contains high levels of nicotine, which it delivers in a highly absorbable form. And nicotine can have considerable impacts on human health. For example, it harms the fetus, so pregnant and breastfeeding mothers do well to avoid consuming any form of nicotine, including Nordic snus.

Here, it is important to note that some tobacco companies currently market a product called "snus," also known as "American snus," without specifying how they produce it or what it contains. This makes it difficult to know whether or not they use pasteurized tobacco, for example. In contrast to Nordic snus, American snus contains sugar and relatively low levels of readily absorbable nicotine; as such, it seems designed to complement cigarette smoking, rather than replace it. Chemical analysis shows that American snus contains on average twice the amounts of nitrosamines contained in Nordic snus.[19] But for the moment, the secrecy surrounding the production of American snus makes it difficult to know the true nature of this product.

RAPÉ

Last but not least, *rapé*. This nasal snuff from South America has recently gained international popularity. Indigenous Amazonian people have prepared *rapé* in different forms for millennia, using it for various medicinal, ritualistic, and social purposes. *Rapé* tends to be made from *Nicotiana rustica* and therefore contains high levels of nicotine. It may also contain alkaline ashes, which increase the availability of nicotine, as well as other plant materials, such as cinnamon and cacao, for flavor.

To date, only one study has examined the chemical composition of different *rapés,* based on a sample of ten commercial products purchased in Brazil and two *rapés* handmade by indigenous Amazonians. Remarkably, the nitrosamine levels of the handmade *rapés* were similar to those of Nordic snus, whereas the commercial *rapés* had nitrosamine levels that were on average fifteen times higher. The researchers attributed this difference to the use of fermented tobacco by the commercial brands. However, the two indigenous *rapés* had higher levels of carcinogenic hydrocarbons in comparison to their commercial counterparts, indicating that they were made with fire-dried tobacco.[20]

One single study involving a total of twelve samples is clearly an insufficient basis for making generalizations. And *rapé* production is completely unregulated, so any given *rapé* may or may not contain fermented or fire-dried tobacco, as well as a number of plant admixtures; like other forms of snuff, *rapé* varies considerably in composition.[21] To date, there have been no studies of its health impacts. All this makes it difficult to assess the risks presented by this South American tobacco product.

More research is needed on *rapé.*

In conclusion, the case of Nordic snus shows that it is possible to reduce the dangers of tobacco products by treating the tobacco plants carefully from start to finish. This includes paying attention to cultivation, processing, and storage, as well as avoiding fermented and fire-dried tobacco. And users probably gain from refrigerating their tobacco products, if possible.

No tobacco or nicotine-containing product can qualify as safe. Tobacco is a powerful plant, and its main alkaloid, nicotine, is a powerful substance. In all cases, tobacco and nicotine need handling with clarity and care.

ACKNOWLEDGMENTS

Thanks to *tabaquera* Corinne Petignat, who accompanied the conception and writing of this book with goodwill and kindness.

Thanks to Eve Berdat for her research assistance.

Thanks to the following readers for their critical feedback: Never Tuesta Cerrón, Barbara Moulton, Gaspar Narby, Luis Eduardo Luna, J. P. Harpignies, Helle Kaasik, Arthur Narby, Eduardo Schenberg, Stéphane Allix, José Marin, Renate Bürgi-Lovis, Stefan Biedermann, Peter Wroblewski, and Lena Vallat.

Thanks to Tigrane Hadengue and Michka of Mama Editions for backing the project from the get-go.

And thanks to Jason Gardner and Kristen Cashman of New World Library for their fantastic work. And to Tanya Fox for her eagle eye.

ENDNOTES

FOREWORD BY GAYLE HIGHPINE

1. Descola, *Spears of Twilight*.
2. Wilbert, *Tobacco and Shamanism in South America*.
3. Rudgley, *Encyclopedia of Psychoactive Substances*, 253.

CHAPTER 1: MEDICINE AND MALICE

1. Gow, *Of Mixed Blood*, 80.

CHAPTER 2: REMEDY AND POISON

1. See Leffingwell, "Chemical Constituents of Tobacco Leaf." For a list of the 599 additives approved by the US government for use in the manufacture of cigarettes, see Benavidez, *Getting High*, 132ff., or Wikipedia

under "List of additives in cigarettes." Additives make up approximately 10 percent of the smokable matter of industrial cigarettes.

2. For a recent list of *Nicotiana* species, see Oyuela-Caycedo and Kawa, "Deep History of Tobacco," 28–31. A majority of *Nicotiana* species are endemic to South America, the continent believed to be the birthplace of human tobacco use — see Oyuela-Caycedo and Kawa, "Deep History of Tobacco," and Berlowitz et al., "Tobacco Is the Chief Medicinal Plant." See Sun et al., "Variations of Alkaloid Accumulation," for an analysis of tobacco's alkaloid content, and Wilbert, *Tobacco and Shamanism*, 137, on nicotine's toxicity. According to Benowitz et al., "Nicotine Chemistry," 30, nicotine comprises 95 percent of the total alkaloid content in commercial cigarette tobacco, and "in most tobacco strains, nornicotine and anatabine are the most abundant of minor alkaloids, followed by anabasine." According to Leffingwell, "Chemical Constituents of Tobacco Leaf," and Charlton, "Medicinal Uses of Tobacco," the effects of tobacco might differ from those of nicotine alone. Most scientific studies focus exclusively on nicotine, but the numerous other substances contained in tobacco may well contribute to its effects — see this chapter's note 23 below.

3. See Ujváry, "Nicotine and Other Insecticidal Alkaloids," and Albuquerque et al., "Mammalian Nicotinic Acetylcholine Receptors," on nicotine's role as an insecticide.

4. See Pendell, *Pharmako/poeia*, 33. See Taghavi et al., "Nicotine Content," on the nicotine content of cigarettes.

5. Le Couteur and Burreson, *Napoleon's Buttons*, 259.

6. Tobacco contains about four thousand different substances, and cigarette manufacturers add about six hundred chemicals to sauce the tobacco; but smoke from a burning industrial cigarette contains more than seven thousand chemicals, at least two hundred fifty of which are known to be harmful, including arsenic, benzene, cadmium, chromium, formaldehyde, hydrogen cyanide, polonium-210, and vinyl chloride. This means that burning cigarettes creates new, often toxic substances — see National Cancer Institute, "Harms of

Cigarette Smoking," and American Lung Association, "What's in a Cigarette?"

7. See Wilbert, *Tobacco and Shamanism*, 46–48, 124.

8. Pendell, *Pharmako/poeia*, 33.

9. See Papke, "Merging Old and New Perspectives," and Changeux, "Nicotinic Acetylcholine Receptor."

10. See Trimarchi and Meeker-O'Connell, "How Nicotine Works."

11. The quote is from Wessler et al., "Non-neuronal Cholinergic System," 2. See also Wessler and Kirkpatrick, "Acetylcholine beyond Neurons"; Albuquerque et al., "Mammalian Nicotinic Acetylcholine Receptors"; Zemkova et al., "Multiple Cholinergic Signaling Pathways"; and Mishra et al., "Harmful Effects of Nicotine."

12. Graham, "Researchers Light Up," and Farsalinos et al., "Nicotine and SARS-CoV-2."

13. The quote is from Perlman, "Nicotine Study Surprises Scientists," 1. See also Graham, "Researchers Light Up."

14. See Farsalinos et al., "Nicotine and SARS-CoV-2" and "Nicotinic Cholinergic System"; Kalra et al., "Immunosuppressive and Anti-inflammatory Effects"; Changeux et al., "Nicotinic Hypothesis for COVID-19"; Tindle et al., "Beyond Smoking Cessation"; Patanavanich and Glantz, "Smoking Is Associated"; Oliveira et al., "Simulations Support the Interaction"; Usman et al., "Is There a Smoker's Paradox?"; Velasquez-Manoff, "How Covid Sends Some Bodies"; and Dance, "Cytokine Storms." The study by Sterne et al., "Association between Administration," confirms that corticosteroids, which stimulate nicotinic receptors, reduce mortality among critically ill patients with Covid-19.

15. Some reports suggest that smokers and vapers face higher Covid-19 danger, in particular teenagers and young adults who vape — see Patanavanich and Glantz, "Smoking Is Associated," and Adams et al., "Medical Vulnerability."

16. See Carlson and Kraus, "Physiology, Cholinergic Receptors"; Quik et al., "Nicotine and Parkinson's Disease"; Newhouse et al., "Nicotine Treatment"; and Koukouli et al., "Nicotine Reverses Hypofrontality."

The latter suggest that nicotine stimulates receptors in brain areas where schizophrenia causes decreased activity. Iha et al., "Nicotine Elicits Convulsive Seizures," and US Food and Drug Administration, "Some E-Cigarette Users," link nicotine to seizures.

17. See Benowitz, "Nicotine and Postoperative Management"; Ditre et al., "Acute Analgesic Effects"; and Wilbert, "Does Pharmacology Corroborate."

18. Spinella, *Pharmacology of Herbal Medicine*, 187. See also Valentine and Sofuoglu, "Cognitive Effects of Nicotine"; Newhouse et al., "Nicotine Treatment"; Heishman et al., "Meta-analysis of the Acute Effects"; and Leary, "Researchers Investigate."

19. The quote is from Wang et al., "Cigarette Smoking," 575. See also Shiels et al., "Association of Cigarette Smoking."

20. Brand et al., "Cigarette Smoking," 3187. It is important to note that increased levels of circulating estrogens are strongly associated with increased risk for breast cancer in postmenopausal women — see Travis and Key, "Oestrogen Exposure."

21. Cross et al., "Sex-Dependent Effects," 432, 430.

22. Wilbert, "Does Pharmacology Corroborate," 185.

23. Janiger and Dobkin de Rios, "*Nicotiana* an Hallucinogen?" reported the presence of small amounts of harmala alkaloids harman and nor-harman in commercial tobaccos and their smoke, with the amounts in smoke forty to one hundred times greater than those in the tobacco leaf. They proposed that these alkaloids might explain the hallucinogenic effects of shamanic tobacco. The presence of harman and norharman in tobacco smoke was confirmed by Herraiz and Chaparro, "Human Monoamine Oxidase," who suggested that these substances may contribute to smoked tobacco's antidepressant-like and neuroprotective effects. However, Sisson and Severson, "Alkaloid Composition," did not report these alkaloids in a sample of sixty-four *Nicotiana* species, nor did Sun et al., "Variations of Alkaloid Accumulation," who studied the alkaloid content of three varieties of *Nicotiana tabacum*.

24. Rätsch, *Encyclopedia of Psychoactive Plants*, 388.

25. Fortier, *"Le Façonnement Neuropharmacologique,"* 135.
26. The quotes are respectively from Lagrou, "Sorcery and Shamanism," 262; Shepard, "Psychoactive Plants," 325; Barbira Freedman, "Shamanic Plants and Gender," 151–52; and Lenaerts, "Substances, Relationship," 11.
27. See Daly and Shepard, "Magic Darts," 15, who discuss the Amazonian concept of medicines as poisons.
28. See Noorani, "Making Psychedelics into Medicines," and Derrida, *Dissemination.*
29. Luna, "Concept of Plants as Teachers," 135.
30. See Jauregui et al., *"Plantas con madre."*
31. Tupper and Labate, "Ayahuasca, Psychedelic Studies," 76.
32. See Lenaerts, "Substances, Relationship," 2, 12, and Lenaerts, *Anthropologie des Indiens Ashéninka d'Amazonie,* 156.
33. Never Tuesta Cerrón, personal email exchange with author, 2020, translated into English by author.
34. Daly and Shepard, "Magic Darts," 14.
35. See McGonigle, "Spirits and Molecules," and Tresca et al., "Evaluating Herbal Medicine Preparation."
36. Viveiros de Castro, "Perspectivism and Multinaturalism," 42.
37. Barbira Freedman, "Shamanic Plants and Gender," 151.
38. See Hornberg, "Animism, Fetishism, and Objectivism."
39. See Kumar, "Revealing *Manduca sexta*'s Nicotine Metabolism."
40. See Leonard, "Can You Overdose," on nicotine overdose from electronic cigarettes, patches, and gum; Wang et al., "E-Cigarette-Induced Pulmonary Inflammation," and Gotts et al., "What Are the Respiratory Effects," on electronic cigarettes and lung inflammation; US Food and Drug Administration, "Some E-Cigarette Users," on electronic cigarettes and seizures; and McBride et al., "Green Tobacco Sickness."

CHAPTER 3: TWO-SIDED PURGE

1. Like other people in the north of the Peruvian Amazon, Rafael Chanchari called one of the plants added to the brew yagé; whereas,

in neighboring Colombia, people use the word *yagé*, or *yajé*, to refer to the ayahuasca vine itself, as well as to the brew made from it. This can be confusing for outsiders.

CHAPTER 4: DISCOMBOBULATING THERAPEUTIC COCKTAIL

1. See Mann, *1493*, 210–13.

2. For a recent list of *Nicotiana* species, see Oyuela-Caycedo and Kawa, "Deep History of Tobacco," 28–31.

3. On ayahuasca varieties identified by Amazonian people, see, for example, Luna, *Vegetalismo*, 151; Langdon, "Siona Classification of Yagé"; Callaway et al., "Phytochemical Analyses," 146; and Weiskopf, *Yajé, the New Purgatory*, 129.

4. Schultes, "Avenues for Future Ethnobotanical Research," 261, and "Recognition of Variability," 229, respectively.

5. De Oliveira et al., "Urgent Need to Review," 2.

6. For an interesting discussion of Schultes's "enigma," see Sheldrake, "The 'Enigma' of Richard Schultes"; Highpine, "Unravelling the Mystery," 29, suggests doing genetic studies of ayahuasca varieties.

7. Rivier and Lindgren, "'Ayahuasca,'" analyzed nine ayahuasca samples, three of which did not contain DMT, and Callaway, "Various Alkaloid Profiles," found one ayahuasca sample out of twenty-nine with no DMT. McKenna et al., "Monoamine Oxidase Inhibitors," formulated the DMT-centered explanation.

8. Davis, *Shadows in the Sun*, 163.

9. The quotes are from Spruce, "On Some Remarkable Narcotics," 184, and Reichel-Dolmatoff, "Cultural Context of an Aboriginal Hallucinogen," 89, 91–92. Spruce drank a single cup of vine-only ayahuasca, then accepted a large calabash of mandioca beer, as well as "a large cigar, two feet long, and as thick as the wrist," from which he took a few puffs, and finally a cup of palm wine. He reported feeling nausea, which he overcame by lying in a hammock and drinking a cup of

coffee. Spruce's Tukano hosts did not seem to have strict *dieta* require-ments at the time.

10. Highpine, "Unravelling the Mystery," 9.

11. See Politi, "Drinking Ayahuasca without DMT," 6, and Shulgin and Shulgin, *TIHKAL*, 446, for reports of harmaline ingestion; and Naranjo, "Psychotropic Properties," 389–90, on harmaline-induced imagery. See also Politi et al., "Traditional Use of *Banisteriopsis caapi*."

12. Callaway, "Phytochemistry and Neuropharmacology," 267.

13. Schenberg et al., "Acute Biphasic Effects," 20–21, found harmine and harmaline to have specific effects in the human electroencephalogram (EEG), implying they contribute to the psychoactive effects of aya-huasca in the brain. Dos Santos et al., "What Mental Health Profes-sionals," 106, discuss the "entourage" effect of ayahuasca's alkaloids. Shulgin and Shulgin, *TIHKAL*, 455–56, provide reports of harmine's effects. Beyer, *Singing to the Plants*, 218, mentions the interactions of the vine's alkaloids.

14. See dos Santos and Hallak, "Effects of the Natural β-Carboline Alka-loid"; Morales-García et al., "Alkaloids of *Banisteriopsis caapi*"; and Ferraz et al., "Pre-clinical Investigations." Regarding Parkinson's dis-ease, pre-clinical studies support using vine-only extracts to improve motor function in patients — see Schwarz et al., "Activities of Extract," and Djamshidian et al., "*Banisteriopsis caapi*."

15. Millard, "Broad Spectrum Roles," 91–92.

16. See Frecska et al., "Therapeutic Potentials of Ayahuasca," 5, who write: "Ayahuasca's high content of bioactive materials points toward a com-bined mechanism of the various effects and calls for further clinical research to reveal the detailed pharmacology of the constituents."

17. See Highpine, "Unravelling the Mystery," 8–9, who mentions learning to "be undistracted by any amount of DMT fireworks" (10). See also Beyer, *Singing to the Plants*, 217, who refers to DMT visions as "side effects" (209).

18. See, for example, Wang et al., "Composition, Standardization," whose research aims to standardize extracts of ayahuasca vines — and who

end up presenting detailed and interesting results concerning the bio-active compounds contained in the vine.

19. See Ott, *Ayahuasca Analogues*, 19–31; the quote is on page 19.

20. Torres, "Origin of the Ayahuasca/Yagé Concept," 238.

21. See Kaasik et al., "Chemical Composition"; the quote is from a personal communication with Kaasik in 2020.

22. See Wang et al., "Composition, Standardization," on the vine's chemical complexity.

23. Kaasik (personal communication in 2020) found traces of the pharmaceutical antidepressant moclobemide in several samples of phony European "ayahuasca."

24. Malcolm and Lee, "Ayahuasca," 43: "Ayahuasca has a complex pharmacologic mechanism that is not yet fully elucidated." Dos Santos and Hallak, "Ayahuasca, an Ancient Substance," 4: "The neural basis and mechanism of action of the therapeutic effect of serotonergic hallucinogens are not yet fully understood."

25. Pollan, *How to Change Your Mind*, provides a readable summary of this research.

26. Dos Santos et al., "What Mental Health Professionals," 107: "Compared to other hallucinogens such as psilocybin, neuroimaging studies with ayahuasca are still small in number, but this picture should change in the near future since there is an increasing number of studies with ayahuasca." See Araujo et al., "Seeing with the Eyes Shut," on the brain areas stimulated by ayahuasca.

27. See Labate and Cavnar, *Therapeutic Use of Ayahuasca*; Frecska et al., "Therapeutic Potentials of Ayahuasca"; Talin and Sanabria, "Ayahuasca's Entwined Efficacy"; Pollan, *How to Change Your Mind*; and Palhano-Fontes et al., "Rapid Antidepressant Effects."

28. In their reports, scientific researchers describe ayahuasca as "typically obtained by decoction of two plants from the Amazonian flora: the bush *Psychotria viridis*, which contains DMT, and the liana *Banisteriopsis caapi*, that contains MAOIs" (Viol et al., "Shannon Entropy," 2), or they refer to the batch they have analyzed as "a standard

sample ... consisting of the stalks of *B. caapi* (rich in harmine, THH, and harmaline) combined with the washed leaves of *P. viridis* (rich in DMT), boiled and concentrated for several hours" (Osório et al., "Antidepressant Effects"). Uthaug et al., "Sub-acute and Long-Term Effects," 2979, give the following definition of the brew: "Ayahuasca is prepared from the *Psychotria viridis* bush that contains the seroto-nergic 2A receptor agonist N,N-dimethyltryptamine (DMT) and the *Banisteriopsis caapi* liana that contains β-carboline alkaloids such as harmine, harmaline and tetrahydroharmine." Schenberg et al., "Acute Biphasic Effects," are a notable exception in this DMT-centered trend; by understanding from the start that the ayahuasca vine and its alka-loids play a role in the brew's effects on the brain, they looked for, and found, psychoactive effects of harmine and harmaline by EEG mea-surement.

29. See dos Santos, "Safety and Side Effects," and dos Santos et al., "Anti-depressive, Anxiolytic," 195, 204.

30. See Hamill et al., "Ayahuasca," 9; Malcolm and Lee, "Ayahuasca," 41; dos Santos, "Safety and Side Effects," 71; and dos Santos, "Critical Eval-uation of Reports."

31. Regarding the lethal dose, see Malcolm and Lee, "Ayahuasca," 40, and dos Santos and Hallak, "Ayahuasca, an Ancient Substance," 5. Dos Santos, "Safety and Side Effects," 70, refers to "a standard dose of aya-huasca of 2 mL/kg body weight"; this implies a dose of 100 mL for a 50 kg adult woman; 20 times this amount is 2 liters. Of course, ayahuasca can be boiled down into a thick and potent syrup, and in such cases, the average effective dose becomes smaller; Kaasik et al., "Chemical Com-position," 10, gives 25 mL as the "usual ceremonial dose" for women served at Santo Daime churches in Brazil — in this case, 20 times the amount would be half a liter, which remains a difficult amount of aya-huasca syrup to swallow and keep down.

32. See Frecska et al., "Possibly Sigma-1 Receptor Mediated"; Frecska et al., "Therapeutic Potentials of Ayahuasca"; and Szabo et al., "Endoge-nous Hallucinogen."

33. Malcolm and Lee, "Ayahuasca," 41, and Hamill et al., "Ayahuasca," 7, state that ayahuasca is not addictive. For the possible brain mechanisms, see Prickett and Liester, "Hypotheses Regarding Ayahuasca's Potential Mechanisms," 117–18.

34. See Prickett and Liester, "Hypotheses Regarding Ayahuasca's Potential Mechanisms," 120–21.

35. See dos Santos and Hallak, "Effects of the Natural β-Carboline Alkaloid," and Uthaug et al., "Sub-acute and Long-Term Effects."

36. See Jiménez-Garrido et al., "Effects of Ayahuasca," and Sanches et al., "Antidepressant Effects."

37. See Kilham, *Ayahuasca Test Pilots Handbook*, 137–38; Harris, *Listening to Ayahuasca*, 145–49; and Sanches et al., "Antidepressant Effects," 80.

38. Dos Santos et al., "Ayahuasca, Dimethyltryptamine," 153. See also Frecska, "Therapeutic Guidelines," 77.

39. Luna, "Some Observations," 277.

40. See Hearn, "Dark Side of Ayahuasca," and Peluso, "Ayahuasca's Attractions and Distractions." On the enhancement of suggestibility by hallucinogens, which can be used and abused, see Dobkin de Rios and Grob, *Hallucinogens, Suggestibility, and Adolescence.*

41. Harris, *Listening to Ayahuasca*, 167. See also Chacruna Institute of Psychedelic Plant Medicines' publication of "*Ayahuasca Community Guidelines for the Awareness of Sexual Abuse*," which notes: "Sexual abuse and misconduct towards female participants in ayahuasca circles are, unfortunately, quite prevalent. Exact numbers are difficult to obtain, as most cases never come to light; nonetheless, the issue is common knowledge within the ayahuasca community." This online document lists a number of useful safety guidelines.

42. Gow, *An Amazonian Myth*, 139, writes: "When I asked Piro people why they liked to take ayahuasca, they gave two characteristic replies. Firstly, they said that it was good to vomit, and that ayahuasca cleansed the body of the residues of game that had been eaten. These accumulate over time, causing a generalized malaise and tiredness, and eventually a desire to die. Ayahuasca expels these from the body,

and makes the drinker feel vital and youthful again. Secondly, people told me that it was good to take ayahuasca because it makes you see: as one man put it, 'You can see everything, everything.'"

43. See Alomar et al., "In Vitro Evaluation," and di Giorgio et al., "In Vitro Activity."

44. Nausea and vomiting are the most common "adverse effects" reported in the scientific literature on ayahuasca. See, for example, dos Santos et al., "What Mental Health Professionals," 105; dos Santos and Hallak, "Ayahuasca," 3; and Osório et al., "Antidepressant Effects," 16, 18. Regarding the use of freeze-dried ayahuasca, see, for example, Riba et al., "Effects of the South American Psychoactive," and Osório et al., "Antidepressant Effects," 18. Osório et al. write, "In future studies, it would be interesting to try to reduce the emetic effect of ayahuasca by premedicating with an antiemetic.... Another possibility could be to administer ayahuasca in different formulations. Freeze-dried aya-huasca appears to produce less vomiting than oral ayahuasca" (18). Scientists originally freeze-dried ayahuasca to mask its taste and do double-blind studies with a placebo; they went on to find that in freeze-dried form, ayahuasca induces less vomiting, perhaps because the foul taste is avoided, and perhaps because the liquid in the brew contributes to the vomiting.

45. See Fotiou and Gearin, "Purging and the Body."

46. See Tresca et al., "Evaluating Herbal Medicine Preparation."

47. Viveiros de Castro, "Relative Native," 489. He also writes: "The refusal to pose the question in terms of belief seems to me a critical anthro-pological decision" (491).

48. See Shanon, *Antipodes of the Mind*, 165–66, 195–96.

49. Tim Ingold, "Rethinking the Animate," views animism as "a way of being that is alive and open to a world in continuous birth," rather than "a system of beliefs" (9–10). In "Animism, Fetishism, and Ob-jectivism," Alf Hornburg writes, "In this framework, a more strictly defined category of animism would be reserved for the intermediate and quite reasonable assumption that *all living things are subjects*, i.e.

equipped with a certain capacity for perception, communication, and agency" (29). In *Animism*, Graham Harvey writes: "Animists are people who recognize that the world is full of persons, only some of whom are human, and that life is always lived in relationship with others" (xi).

50. See, for example, Harris, *Listening to Ayahuasca.*

51. Anthropologist Françoise Barbira Freedman, ("Shamanic Plants and Gender," 170), who studied the gendering of shamanic plants in the Upper Amazon, confirms an *"absence of gendering"* of the ayahuasca vine by the indigenous people of the Peruvian Amazon. Furthermore, Amazonian myths and stories portray ayahuasca sometimes as a man, other times as a woman; for example, Cashinahua, Witoto, and Yagua people view the guardian or mother of ayahuasca as a man, while Piro, Canelos Quichua, and Desana people say she is a woman — see respectively Lagrou, "Cashinahua Cosmovision," 116, 120; Niño, "Un-ámarai, Father of Yajé" (quoted in Luna and White, *Ayahuasca Reader*, 100); Chaumeil, *Voir, Savoir, Pouvoir*, 40; Gow, *An Amazonian Myth*, 142; Whitten, *Sacha Runa*, 40; and Reichel-Dolmatoff, *Amazonian Cosmos*, 36–37; and *The Shaman and the Jaguar*, 146ff. Anthropologist Evgenia Fotiou ("From Medicine Men to Day Trippers," 148–49) pointed out the recent trend among Western ayahuasca users to feminize the plant and brew.

APPENDIX: VAPE, SNUFF, *RAPÉ*, AND SNUS

1. See Jones, "Vaping"; Rostron et al., "Smokeless Tobacco Use"; and Fisher et al., "Smokeless Tobacco Mortality Risks."

2. See Zhu et al., "Four Hundred and Sixty Brands," and Muthumalage et al., "Inflammatory and Oxidative Responses."

3. See Orellana-Barrios et al., "Electronic Cigarettes."

4. See Allen et al., "Flavoring Chemicals in E-Cigarettes"; National Academies of Sciences, Engineering, and Medicine, *Public Health Consequences of E-Cigarettes*; Centers for Disease Control and Prevention,

"Flavorings-Related Lung Disease"; and Park et al., "Transcriptional Response."

5. The quote is from Harvard T. H. Chan School of Public Health, "Common E-Cigarette Chemical Flavorings."

6. See Kosmider et al., "Carbonyl Compounds." Hahn et al., "Electronic Cigarettes," found that e-liquids contain on average 37 percent glycerine (or glycerol) and 57 percent propylene glycol.

7. See Flora et al., "Method for the Determination."

8. Olmedo et al., "Metal Concentrations."

9. See National Academies of Sciences, Engineering, and Medicine, *Public Health Consequences of E-Cigarettes*, 203, and Tchounwou et al., "Heavy Metals Toxicity," 2.

10. See Lerner et al., "Electronic Cigarette Aerosols," 624.

11. E-cigarettes may be understood as "electronic nicotine delivery systems" (see, for example, Unger and Unger, "E-Cigarettes"), but they do not always deliver nicotine. One recent study showed that one-third of eighteen-year-olds in the United States had vaped at least once, and among those who had vaped, two-thirds reported vaping "just flavorings," with only 20 percent vaping nicotine and 6 percent vaping cannabis (see Miech et al., "What Are Kids Vaping?").

12. See Wu, "Vaping Links to Covid-19 Risk," and Adams et al., "Medical Vulnerability of Young Adults."

13. See OncoLink Team, "Smokeless Tobacco and Health Risks." The amount of nicotine in the bloodstream after snuff use may be higher than that of a cigarette smoker, and the nicotine may stay in the bloodstream longer, but smoking delivers nicotine to the blood *faster* than any other means of administration — see Benowitz et al., "Nicotine Chemistry."

14. See Hecht, "It Is Time to Regulate," and Mayo Clinic staff, "Chewing Tobacco." Connolly and Saxner, "Informational Update Research," report that the nitrosamine levels in some brands of snuff more than double after six months on the shelf at room temperature. Regarding industrial cigarettes, the presence of nitrosamines varies from none at

all to significantly high levels — see Wu et al., "Determination of Carcinogenic," and Edwards et al., "Tobacco-Specific Nitrosamines" — and e-cigarettes also generate nitrosamines in concentrations that vary from extremely low to quite significant, depending on the temperature of the heating coil, according to Kim and Shin, "Determination of Tobacco-Specific," who call for further studies on the subject.

15. See Mayo Clinic staff, "Chewing Tobacco"; American Cancer Society, "Health Risks of Smokeless Tobacco"; Muthukrishnan and Warnakulasuriya, "Oral Health Consequences"; and Wyss et al., "Smokeless Tobacco Use."

16. See Lawler et al., "Chemical Analysis," and Connolly and Saxner, "Informational Update Research." On limiting nitrogen supply to tobacco plants during cultivation in order to reduce their nitrosamine content during curing, see Castelli et al., "Reduced N Supply."

17. Carlsson et al., "Physiology, Cholinergic Receptors," 405. Regarding the inconclusive nature of scientific studies of Nordic snus's impacts on human health, initial research linked it to higher incidence of oral cancer and pancreatic cancer, but recent large-scale reviews — such as Gakidos et al., "Global, Regional, and National," and Araghi et al., "Use of Moist Oral Snuff" — do not find evidence to support such claims. In the case of insulin resistance, nicotine changes chemical processes in our cells in a way that makes them less responsive to insulin, which they need to take glucose out of the blood to use for energy; this causes sugar to build up in the blood, which can eventually lead to type 2 diabetes.

18. See Foulds et al., "Effect of Smokeless Tobacco."

19. See Lawler et al., "Chemical Analysis of Snus Products."

20. See Stanfill et al., "Comprehensive Chemical Characterization." This study also included two nontobacco commercial *rapés*, which we do not consider in this discussion.

21. See Oldham et al., "Variability of TSNA," on the variability of snuff contents.

BIBLIOGRAPHY

Adams, Sally H., et al. "Medical Vulnerability of Young Adults to Severe COVID-19 Illness: Data from the National Health Interview Survey." *Journal of Adolescent Health* 67 (2020): 362–68. http://doi.org/10.1016/j.jadohealth.2020.06.025.

Albuquerque, Edson X., et al. "Mammalian Nicotinic Acetylcholine Receptors: From Structure to Function." *Physiological Review* 89, no. 1 (2009): 73–120. http://doi.org/10.1152/physrev.00015.2008.

Allen, Joseph G., et al. "Flavoring Chemicals in E-Cigarettes: Diacetyl, 2,3-Pentanedione, and Acetoin in a Sample of 51 Products, including Fruit-, Candy-, and Cocktail-Flavored E-Cigarettes." *Environmental Health Perspectives* 124, no. 6 (2016): 733–39. http://doi.org/10.1289/ehp.1510185.

Alomar, M. L., et al. "In Vitro Evaluation of β-Carboline Alkaloids as Potential Anti-toxoplasma Agents." *BMC Research Notes* 6 (2013): 193. http://doi.org/10.1186/1756-0500-6-193.

American Cancer Society. "Health Risks of Smokeless Tobacco." 2015. https://www.cancer.org/cancer/cancer-causes/tobacco-and-cancer/smokeless-tobacco.html.

American Lung Association. "What's in a Cigarette?" Updated July 13, 2020. https://www.lung.org/quit-smoking/smoking-facts/whats-in-a-cigarette.

Araghi, Marzieh, et al. "Use of Moist Oral Snuff (Snus) and Pancreatic Cancer: Pooled Analysis of Nine Prospective Observational Studies." *International Journal of Cancer* 141, no. 4 (2017): 687–93. http://doi.org/10.1002/ijc.30773.

Araujo, Draulio B., et al. "Seeing with the Eyes Shut: Neural Basis of Enhanced Imagery following Ayahuasca Ingestion." *Human Brain Mapping* 33 (2012): 2550–60. http://doi.org/10.1002/hbm.21381.

Barbira Freedman, Françoise. "Shamanic Plants and Gender in the Healing Forest." In *Plants, Health, and Healing: On the Interface of Ethnobotany and Medical Anthropology*, edited by Elisabeth Hsu and Stephen Harris, 135–78. Oxford: Berghahn Books, 2010.

Benavidez, Edward J. *Getting High: The Effects of Drugs*. Bloomington, ID: XLIBRIS Corporation, 2013.

Benowitz, Neal L. "Nicotine and Postoperative Management of Pain." *Anesthesia & Analgesia* 107, no. 3 (2008): 739–41. http://doi.org/10.1213/ane.0b013e3181813508.

Benowitz, Neal L., et al. "Nicotine Chemistry, Metabolism, Kinetics, and Biomarkers." *Handbook of Experimental Pharmacology* 192 (2009): 29–60. http://doi.org/10.1007/978-3-540-69248-5_2.

Berlowitz, Ilana, et al. "Tobacco Is the Chief Medicinal Plant in My Work: Therapeutic Uses of Tobacco in Peruvian Amazonian Medicine Exemplified by the Work of a *Maestro Tabaquero*." *Frontiers in Pharmacology* 11 (2020): 594591. http://doi.org/10.3389/fphar.2020.594591.

Beyer, Stephan V. *Singing to the Plants: A Guide to Mestizo Shamanism in the Upper Amazon*. Albuquerque: University of New Mexico Press, 2009.

Brand, Judith S., et al. "Cigarette Smoking and Endogenous Sex Hormones in Postmenopausal Women." *Journal of Clinical Endocrinology & Metabolism* 96, no. 10 (2011): 3184–92. http://doi.org/10.1210/jc.2011-1165.

Callaway, Jace C. "Phytochemistry and Neuropharmacology of Ayahuasca." In *Ayahuasca: Hallucinogens, Consciousness, and the Spirit of Nature*, edited by Ralph Metzner, 250–75. New York: Thunder's Mouth Press, 1999.

———. "Various Alkaloid Profiles in Decoctions of *Banisteriopsis caapi*." *Journal of Psychoactive Drugs* 37, no. 2 (2005): 151–55.

Callaway, Jace C., et al. "Phytochemical Analyses of *Banisteriopsis caapi* and *Psychotria viridis*." *Journal of Psychoactive Drugs* 37, no. 2 (2005): 145–50.

Carlson, Adlei B., and Gregory P. Kraus. "Physiology, Cholinergic Receptors." *StatPearls*. October 27, 2018. https://pubmed.ncbi.nlm.nih.gov/30252390.

Carlsson, Sofia, et al. "Smokeless Tobacco (Snus) Is Associated with an Increased Risk of Type 2 Diabetes: Results from Five Pooled Cohorts." *Journal of Internal Medicine* 281, no. 4 (2017): 398–406. http://doi.org/10.1111/joim.12592.

Castelli, Fabio, Enrico Ceotto, and Renato Contillo. "Reduced N Supply Limits the Nitrate Content of Flue-Cured Tobacco." *Agronomy for Sustainable Development* 31 (2011): 329–35. http://doi.org/10.1051/agro/2010033.

Centers for Disease Control and Prevention. "Flavorings-Related Lung Disease." 2017. https://www.cdc.gov/niosh/topics/flavorings/default.html.

Chacruna Institute of Psychedelic Plant Medicines. "Ayahuasca Community Guidelines for the Awareness of Sexual Abuse." 2019. https//:chacruna.net/community/ayahuasca-community-guide-for-the-awareness-of-sexual-abuse.

Changeux, Jean-Pierre. "The Nicotinic Acetylcholine Receptor: The

Founding Father of the Pentameric Ligand-Gated Ion Channel Superfamily." *Journal of Biological Chemistry* 287, no. 48 (2012): 40207–15. http://doi.org/10.1074/jbc.R112.407668.

Changeux, Jean-Pierre, et al. "A Nicotinic Hypothesis for COVID-19 with Preventive and Therapeutic Implications." *Qeios* (2020): FXGQSB.2. http://doi.org/10.32388/FXGQSB.2.

Charlton, Anne. "Medicinal Uses of Tobacco in History." *Journal of the Royal Society of Medicine* 97 (2004): 292–96.

Chaumeil, Jean-Pierre. *Voir, Savoir, Pouvoir: Le Chamanisme chez les Yagua du Nord-Est Péruvien.* Paris: Editions de l'Ecole des Hautes Etudes en Sciences Sociales, 1983.

Connolly, Gregory N., and Howard Saxner. "Informational Update: Research on Tobacco Specific Nitrosamines (TSNAs) in Oral Snuff and a Request to Tobacco Manufacturers to Voluntarily Set Tolerance Limits for TSNAs in Oral Snuff." Memorandum to Massachusetts Public Health Council. August 21, 2001. https://www.industry documents.ucsf.edu/tobacco/docs/#id=yxvk0150.

Cross, Sarah J., et al. "Sex-Dependent Effects of Nicotine on the Developing Brain." *Journal of Neuroscience Research* 95, nos. 1–2 (2017): 422–36. http://doi.org/10.1002/jnr.23878.

Daly, Lewis, and Glenn Shepard Jr. "Magic Darts and Messenger Molecules: Toward a Phytoethnography of Indigenous Amazonia." *Anthropology Today* 35, no. 2 (2019): 13–17. http://doi.org/10.1111 /1467-8322.12494.

Dance, Amber. "Cytokine Storms: When the Body Attacks Itself." BBC Future. May 7, 2020. https://www.bbc.com/future/article /20200505-cytokine-storms-when-the-body-attacks-itself.

Davis, Wade. *Shadows in the Sun: Travels to Landscapes of Spirit and Desire.* Washington, DC: Island Press, 1998.

De Oliveira, Regina Celia, et al. "The Urgent Need to Review the Botanical Classification of the Ayahuasca Vine." 2018. https://chacruna.net /urgent-botanical-classification-ayahuasca.

Derrida, Jacques. *Dissemination*. Chicago: University of Chicago Press, 1981.

Descola, Philippe. *The Spears of Twilight: Life and Death in the Amazon Jungle*. Translated by Janet Lloyd. New York: New Press, 1996.

Di Giorgio, C., et al. "In Vitro Activity of the β-Carboline Alkaloids Harmane, Harmine, and Harmaline toward Parasites of the Species *Leishmania infantum*." *Experimental Parasitology* 106, nos. 3–4 (2004): 67–74. http://doi.org/10.1016/j.exppara.2004.04.002.

Ditre, Joseph W., et al. "Acute Analgesic Effects of Nicotine and Tobacco in Humans: A Meta-analysis." *Pain* 157, no. 7 (2016): 1373–81. http://doi.org/10.1097/j.pain.0000000000000572.

Djamshidian, Atbin, et al. "*Banisteriopsis caapi*: A Forgotten Potential Therapy for Parkinson's Disease?" *Movement Disorders Clinical Practice* 3 (2015): 19–26. http://doi.org/10.1002/mdc3.12242.

Dobkin de Rios, Marlene, and Charles Grob. *Hallucinogens, Suggestibility, and Adolescence in Cross-Cultural Perspective*. Berlin: VWB Verlag, 1995.

Dos Santos, Rafael G. "A Critical Evaluation of Reports Associating Ayahuasca with Life-Threatening Adverse Reactions." *Journal of Psychoactive Drugs* 45, no. 2 (2013): 179–88. http://doi.org/10.1080/02791072.2013.785846.

———. "Safety and Side Effects of Ayahuasca in Humans: An Overview Focusing on Developmental Toxicology." *Journal of Psychoactive Drugs* 45, no. 1 (2013): 68–78. http://doi.org/10.1080/02791072.2013.763564.

Dos Santos, Rafael G., and Jaime E. C. Hallak. "Effects of the Natural β-Carboline Alkaloid Harmine, a Main Constituent of Ayahuasca, in Memory and in the Hippocampus: A Systematic Literature Review of Preclinical Studies." *Journal of Psychoactive Drugs* 49, no. 1 (2017): 1–10. http://doi.org/10.1080/02791072.2016.1260189.

———. "Ayahuasca, an Ancient Substance with Traditional and Contemporary Use in Neuropsychiatry and Neuroscience." *Epilepsy & Behavior* 106300 (2019). http://doi.org/10.1016/j.yebeh.2019.04.053.

Dos Santos, Rafael G., et al. "Antidepressive, Anxiolytic, and Antiaddictive Effects of Ayahuasca, Psilocybin, and Lysergic Acid Diethylamide (LSD): A Systematic Review of Clinical Trials Published in the Last 25 Years." *Therapeutic Advances in Psychopharmacology* 6, no. 3 (2016): 193–213. http://doi.org/10.1177/2045125316638008.

———. "Ayahuasca, Dimethyltryptamine, and Psychosis: A Systematic Review of Human Studies." *Therapeutic Advances in Psychopharmacology* 7, no. 4 (2017): 141–57. http://doi.org/10.1177/2045125316689030.

———. "Ayahuasca: What Mental Health Professionals Need to Know." *Archives of Clinical Psychiatry* 44, no. 4 (2017): 103–9. http://doi.org/10.1590/0101-60830000000130.

Edwards, Selvin H., et al. "Tobacco-Specific Nitrosamines in the Tobacco and Mainstream Smoke of US Commercial Cigarettes." *Chemical Research in Toxicology* 30, no. 2 (2017): 540–51. http://doi.org/10.1021/acs.chemrestox.6b00268.

Farsalinos, Konstantinos, et al. "Editorial: Nicotine and SARS-CoV-2: COVID-19 May Be a Disease of the Nicotinic Cholinergic System." *Toxicology Reports* 7 (2020): 658–63. http://doi.org/10.1016/j.toxrep.2020.04.012.

———. "Nicotinic Cholinergic System and COVID-19: In Silico Identification of an Interaction between SARS-CoV-2 and Nicotinic Receptors with Potential Therapeutic Targeting Implications." *International Journal of Molecular Sciences* 21 (2020): 5807. http://doi.org/10.3390/ijms21165807.

Ferraz, Christine Adrielly Alves, et al. "Pre-clinical Investigations of β-Carboline Alkaloids as Antidepressant Agents: A Systematic Review." *Fitoterapia* 137 (2019): 104196. http://doi.org/10.1016/j.fitote.2019.104196.

Fisher, Michael T., et al. "Smokeless Tobacco Mortality Risks: An Analysis of Two Contemporary Nationally Representative Longitudinal Mortality Studies." *Harm Reduction Journal* 16 (2019): 27. http://doi.org/10.1186/s12954-019-0294-6.

Flora, Jason W., et al. "Method for the Determination of Carbonyl Compounds in E-Cigarette Aerosols." *Journal of Chromatographic Science* 55, no. 2 (2017): 142–48. http://doi.org/10.1093/chromsci/bmw157.

Fortier, Martin. *"Le Façonnement Neuropharmacologique de la Culture: Anthropologie Comparée des Rituels à Hallucinogènes Sérotoninergiques et Anticholinergiques." Cahiers d'Anthropologie Sociale* 17, no. 2 (2018): 132–51. http://doi.org/10.3917/cas.017.0132.

Fotiou, Evgenia. "From Medicine Men to Day Trippers: Shamanic Tourism in Iquitos, Peru." PhD dissertation in anthropology, University of Wisconsin-Madison, 2010. http://doi.org/10.13140/RG.2.2.29990.32327.

Fotiou, Evgenia, and Alex K. Gearin. "Purging and the Body in the Therapeutic Use of Ayahuasca." *Social Science and Medicine* 239 (2019): 112532. http://doi.org/10:1016/j.socsimed.2019.112532.

Foulds, Jonathan, et al. "Effect of Smokeless Tobacco (Snus) on Smoking and Public Health in Sweden." *Tobacco Control* 12 (2003): 349–59.

Frecska, Ede. "Therapeutic Guidelines: Dangers and Contra-indications in Therapeutic Applications of Hallucinogens." In *Psychedelic Medicine*, edited by Thomas B. Roberts and Michael J. Winkelman, 69–95. New York: Praeger, 2007.

Frecska, Ede, Attila Szabo, Michael James Winkelman, and Luis Eduardo Luna. "A Possibly Sigma-1 Receptor Mediated Role of Dimethyltryptamine in Tissue Protection, Regeneration, and Immunity." *Journal of Neural Transmission* 120 (2013): 1295–303. http://doi.org/10.1007/s00702-013-1024-y.

Frecska, Ede, P. Bokor, and Michael A. Winkelman. "The Therapeutic Potentials of Ayahuasca: Possible Effects against Various Diseases of Civilization." *Frontiers in Pharmacology* 7 (2016). http://doi.org/10.3389/fphar.2016.00035.

Gakidos, Emmanuela, et al. "Global, Regional, and National Comparative Risk Assessment of 84 Behavioural, Environmental and Occupational, and Metabolic Risks or Clusters of Risks, 1990–2016: A Systematic Analysis for the Global Burden of Disease Study 2016." *The Lancet* 390 (2017): 1345–422. http://doi.org/10.1016/S0140-6736(17)32366-8.

Gotts, Jeffrey E., et al. "What Are the Respiratory Effects of E-Cigarettes?" *British Medical Journal* 366 (2019): 15275. http://doi.org/10.1136 /bmj.15275.

Gow, Peter. *Of Mixed Blood: Kinship and History in the Peruvian Amazon*. Oxford: Clarendon Press, 1991.

———. *An Amazonian Myth and Its History*. Oxford: Oxford University Press, 2001.

Graham, Marty. "Researchers Light Up for Nicotine, the Wonder Drug." *Wired* (June 20, 2007). https://www.wired.com/2007/06/nicotine.

Hahn, Jürgen, et al. "Electronic Cigarettes: Overview of Chemical Composition and Exposure Estimation." *Tobacco Induced Diseases* 12 (2014): 23. http://doi.org/10.1186/s12971-014-0023-6.

Hamill, Jonathan, et al. "Ayahuasca: Psychological and Physiologic Effects, Pharmacology, and Potential Uses in Addiction and Mental Illness." *Current Neuropharmacology* 16 (2018): 1–19. http://doi.org/10.2174 /1570158X16666180125095902.

Harris, Rachel. *Listening to Ayahuasca: New Hope for Depression, Addiction, PTSD, and Anxiety.* Novato, CA: New World Library, 2017.

Harvard T. H. Chan School of Public Health. "Common E-Cigarette Chemical Flavorings May Impair Lung Function." 2019. https://www .hsph.harvard.edu/news/press-releases/common-e-cigarette-chemical -flavorings-may-impair-lung-function.

Harvey, Graham. *Animism: Respecting the Living World*. London: Hurst & Co., 2006.

Hearn, Kelly. "The Dark Side of Ayahuasca." *Men's Journal* 22, no. 2 (2013): 38–41.

Hecht, Stephen S. "It Is Time to Regulate Carcinogenic Tobacco-Specific Nitrosamines in Cigarette Tobacco." *Cancer Prevention Research (Phila)* 7, no. 7 (2014): 639–47. http://doi.org/10.1158/1940-6207 .CAPR-14-0095.

Heishman, Stephen, et al. "Meta-analysis of the Acute Effects of Nicotine and Smoking on Human Performance." *Psychopharmacology (Berl.)* 210, no. 4 (2010): 453–69. http://doi.org/10.1007/s00213-010-1848-1.

Herraiz, Tomas, and Carolina Chaparro. "Human Monoamine Oxidase Is Inhibited by Tobacco Smoke: β-Carboline Alkaloids Act as Potent and Reversible Inhibitors." *Biochemical and Biophysical Research Communications* 326 (2005): 378–86. http://doi.org/10.1016/j.bbrc .2004.11.033.

Highpine, Gayle. "Unravelling the Mystery of the Origin of Ayahuasca." 2012. http://www.neip.info/novo/wp-content/uploads/2015/04 /highpine_origin-of-ayahuasca_neip_2012.pdf.

Hornberg, Alf. "Animism, Fetishism, and Objectivism as Strategies for Knowing (or not Knowing) the World." *Ethnos* 7, no. 1 (2006): 21–32. http://doi.org/10.1080/0014840600603129.

Iha, Higor A., et al. "Nicotine Elicits Convulsive Seizures by Activating Amygdalar Neurons." *Frontiers in Pharmacology* 8 (2017): 57. http://doi.org/10.3389/fphar.2017.00057.

Ingold, Tim. "Rethinking the Animate, Re-animating Thought." *Ethnos* 71, no. 1 (2006): 9–20. http://doi.org/10.1080/00141840600603111.

Janiger, Oscar, and Marlene Dobkin de Rios. "*Nicotiana* an Hallucinogen?" *Economic Botany* 30 (1976): 149–51.

Jauregui, X., et al. "*Plantas con madre*: Plants that Teach and Guide in the Shamanic Initiation Process in the East-Central Peruvian Amazon." *Journal of Ethnopharmacology* 134, no. 3 (2011): 739–52. http://doi .org/10.1016/j.jep.2011.01.042.

Jiménez-Garrido, Daniel F., et al. "Effects of Ayahuasca on Mental Health and Quality of Life in Naïve Users: A Longitudinal and Cross-Sectional Study Combination." *Scientific Reports* 10 (2020): 4075. http://doi.org/10.1038/s41598-020-61169-x.

Jones, Lora. "Vaping: How Popular Are E-Cigarettes?" *BBC News* (September 15, 2019). https://www.bbc.com/news/business-44295336.

Kaasik, Helle, et al. "Chemical Composition of Traditional and Analogue Ayahuasca." *Journal of Psychoactive Drugs* (September 8, 2020): 1–11. http://doi.org/10.1080/02791072.2020.1815911.

Kalra, Roma, et al. "Immunosuppressive and Anti-inflammatory Effects of Nicotine Administered by Patch in an Animal Model." *Clinical and Diagnostic Laboratory Immunology* 11, no. 3 (2004): 563–68. http://doi .org/10.1128/CDLI.11.3.563-568.2004.

Kilham, Chris. *The Ayahuasca Test Pilots Handbook: The Essential Guide to Ayahuasca Journeying.* Berkeley, CA: Evolver Editions, 2014.

Kim, Hyun-Ji, and Ho-Sang Shin. "Determination of Tobacco-Specific Nitrosamines in Replacement Liquids of Electronic Cigarettes by Liquid Chromatography-Tandem Mass Spectrometry." *Journal of Chromatography A* 1291 (2013): 48–55. http://doi.org/10.1016/j.chroma .2013.03.035.

Kosmider, Leon, et al. "Carbonyl Compounds in Electronic Cigarette Vapors: Effects of Nicotine Solvent and Battery Output Voltage." *Nicotine & Tobacco Research* 10 (2014): 1319–26. http://doi.org /10.1093/ntr/ntu078.

Koukouli, Fani, et al. "Nicotine Reverses Hypofrontality in Animal Models of Addiction and Schizophrenia." *Nature Medicine* 23 (2017): 347–54. http://doi.org/10.1038/nm.4274.

Kumar, Pavan. "Revealing *Manduca sexta*'s Nicotine Metabolism and Its Ecological Consequences Using Plant Mediated RNAi Based Reverse Genetics." Dissertation, Thüringer Universitäts- und Landesbiblio- thek Jena, 2013. https://d-nb.info/1050978005/34.

Labate, Beatriz Caiuby, and Clancy Canvar, eds. *The Therapeutic Use of Ayahuasca.* Berlin: Springer-Verlag, 2014.

Lagrou, Elsje Maria. "Cashinahua Cosmovision: A Perspectival Approach to Identity and Alterity." Doctoral dissertation, University of St. Andrews, 1998.

———. "Sorcery and Shamanism in Cashinahua Discourse and Praxis, Purus River, Brazil." In *In Darkness and Secrecy: The Anthropology of Assault Sorcery and Witchcraft in Amazonia,* edited by Neil L. Whitehead and Robin Wright, 244–71. Durham, NC: Duke University Press, 2004.

Langdon, E. Jean. "Siona Classification of Yagé: Ethnobotany,

Ethnochemistry, and History." In *Rituales y Fiestas de las Américas*, edited by Elizabeth Reichel D., 328–40. Bogotá: Ediciones Uniandes, 1988.

Lawler, Tameka S., et al. "Chemical Analysis of Snus Products from the United States and Northern Europe." *PLOS ONE* 15, no. 1 (2020): e0227837. http://doi.org/10.1371/journal.pone.0227837.

Leary, Warren E. "Researchers Investigate (Horrors!) Nicotine's Potential Benefits." *New York Times* (January 14, 1997): B11.

Le Couteur, Penny, and Jay Burreson. *Napoleon's Buttons: How 17 Molecules Changed History*. New York: Jeremy P. Tarcher, 2004.

Leffingwell, John C. "Chemical Constituents of Tobacco Leaf and Differences among Tobacco Types." In *Tobacco: Production, Chemistry, and Technology*, edited by D. Layten Davis and Mark T. Nielsen, 265–84. Oxford: Blackwell Science, 1999.

Lenaerts, Marc. *Anthropologie des Indiens Ashéninka d'Amazonie: Nos sœurs Manioc et l'étranger Jaguar*. Paris: L'Harmattan, 2004.

———. "Substances, Relationship, and the Omnipresence of the Body: An Overview of Ashéninka Ethnomedicine (Western Amazonia)." *Journal of Ethnobiology and Ethnomedicine* 2 (2006). http://doi.org/10.1186/1746-4269-2-49.

Leonard, Jayne. "Can You Overdose on Too Much Nicotine?" *MedicalNewsToday* (October 6, 2017). https://www.medicalnewstoday.com/articles/319627.

Lerner, Chad A., et al. "Electronic Cigarette Aerosols and Copper Nanoparticles Induce Mitochondrial Stress and Promote DNA Fragmentation in Lung Fibroblasts." *Biochemical and Biophysical Research Communications* 477, no. 4 (2016): 620–25. http://doi.org/10.1016/j.bbrc.2016.06.109.

Luna, Luis Eduardo. "The Concept of Plants as Teachers among Four Peruvian Shamans of Iquitos, Northeast Peru." *Journal of Ethnopharmacology* 11 (1984): 135–56.

———. *Vegetalismo: Shamanism among the Mestizo Population of the Peruvian Amazon*. Stockholm: Almqvist and Wiskell, 1986.

————. "Some Observations on the Phenomenology of the Ayahuasca Experience." In *Ayahuasca Reader: Encounters with the Sacred Vine*, edited by Luis Eduardo Luna and Steven F. White, 251–79. Santa Fe, NM: Synergistic Press, 2016.

Luna, Luis Eduardo, and Steven F. White, eds. *Ayahuasca Reader: Encounters with the Sacred Vine*. Santa Fe, NM: Synergistic Press, 2016.

Malcolm, Benjamin J., and Kelly C. Lee. "Ayahuasca: An Ancient Sacrament for Treatment of Contemporary Psychiatric Illness?" *Mental Health Clinician* 7, no. 1 (2017): 39–45. http://doi.org/10.9740/mhc.2017.01.039.

Mann, Charles C. *1493: Uncovering the World Columbus Created*. New York: Vintage Books, 2011.

Mayo Clinic staff. "Chewing Tobacco: Not a Safe Product." 2019. https://www.mayoclinic.org/healthy-lifestyle/quit-smoking/in-depth/chewing-tobacco/art-20047428.

McBride, Jeffrey S., et al. "Green Tobacco Sickness." *Tobacco Control* 7 (1998): 294–98.

McGonigle, Ian Vincent. "Spirits and Molecules: Ethnopharmacology and Symmetrical Epistemological Pluralism." *Ethnos* 82, no. 1 (2015): 139–64. http://doi.org/10.1080/00141844.2015.1042490.

McKenna, Dennis J., et al. "Monoamine Oxidase Inhibitors in South American Hallucinogenic Plants: Tryptamine and Beta-Carboline Constituents of Ayahuasca." *Journal of Ethnopharmacology* 10 (1984): 195–223.

Miech, Richard, et al. "What Are Kids Vaping? Results from a National Survey of US Adolescents." *Tobacco Control* 26 (2017): 386–91. http://doi.org/10.1136/tobaccocontrol-2016-053014.

Millard, Dale. "Broad Spectrum Roles of Harmine in Ayahuasca." In *Ethnopharmacological Search for Psychoactive Drugs, II: 50 Years of Research (1967–2017)*, edited by Sir Ghillean Prance, 82–94. Santa Fe, NM: Synergistic Press, 2017.

Mishra, Aseem, et al. "Harmful Effects of Nicotine." *Indian Journal of*

Medical and Paediatric Oncology 36, no. 1 (2015): 24–31. http://doi
.org/10.4103/0971-5851.151771.

Morales-García, Jose A., et al. "The Alkaloids of *Banisteriopsis caapi*, the
Plant Source of the Amazonian Hallucinogen Ayahuasca, Stimulate
Adult Neurogenesis In Vitro." *Scientific Reports* 7 (2017): 5309.
http://doi.org/10.1038/s41598-017-05407-9.

Muthukrishnan, Arvind, and Saman Warnakulasuriya. "Oral Health
Consequences of Smokeless Tobacco Use." *Indian Journal of Medical
Research* 148 (2018): 35–40. http://doi.org/10.4103/ijmr.IJMR_1793_17.

Muthumalage, Thivanka, et al. "Inflammatory and Oxidative Responses
Induced by Exposure to Commonly Used E-Cigarette Flavoring
Chemicals and Flavored E-Liquids without Nicotine." *Frontiers in
Physiology* 8 (2018): 1130. http://doi.org/10.3389/phys.2017.01130.

Naranjo, Claudio. "Psychotropic Properties of the Harmala Alkaloids."
In *Ethnopharmacological Search for Psychoactive Drugs*, edited by
D. H. Efron et al., 385–91. Washington, DC: US Department of
Health, Education, and Welfare, 1967.

National Academies of Sciences, Engineering, and Medicine. *Public
Health Consequences of E-Cigarettes*. Washington, DC: The National
Academies Press, 2018. http://doi.org/10.17226/24952.

National Cancer Institute. "Harms of Cigarette Smoking and Health Benefits of Quitting." Updated December 19, 2017. https://www.cancer.gov
/about-cancer/causes-prevention/risk/tobacco/cessation-fact-sheet.

Newhouse, P., et al. "Nicotine Treatment of Mild Cognitive Impairment:
A 6-Month Double-Blind Pilot Clinical Trial." *Neurology* 78, no. 2
(2012): 91–101. http://doi.org/10.1212/WNL.0b013e31823efcbb.

Niño, Hugo. "Unámarai, Father of Yajé." In *Ayahuasca Reader: Encounters
with the Amazon's Sacred Vine*, edited by Luis Eduardo Luna and
Steven F. White, 100–106. Santa Fe, NM: Synergistic Press, 2016.

Noorani, Tehseen. "Making Psychedelics into Medicines: The Politics and
Paradoxes of Medicalization." *Journal of Psychedelic Studies* 4, no. 1
(2020): 34–39. http://doi.org/10.1556/2054.2019.018.

Oldham, M. J., et al. "Variability of TSNA in US Tobacco and Moist Smokeless Tobacco Products." *Toxicology Reports* 7 (2020): 752–58. http://doi.org/10.1016/j.toxrep.2020.05.008.

Oliveira, A. Sofia F., et al. "Simulations Support the Interaction of the SARS-CoV-2 Spike Protein with Nicotinic Acetylcholine Receptors and Suggest Subtype Specificity." *bioRxiv* (July 16, 2020). http://doi .org/10.1101/2020.07.16.206680.

Olmedo, Pablo, et al. "Metal Concentrations in E-Cigarette Liquid and Aerosol Samples: The Contribution of Metallic Coils." *Environmental Health Perspectives* 26, no. 2 (2018). http://doi.org/10.1289/EHP2175.

OncoLink Team. "Smokeless Tobacco and Health Risks." 2020. https:// www.oncolink.org/risk-and-prevention/smoking-tobacco-and-cancer /smokeless-tobacco-and-health-risks.

Orellana-Barrios, Menfil A., et al. "Electronic Cigarettes: A Narrative Re- view for Clinicians." *American Journal of Medicine* 128, no. 7 (2015): 674–81. http://doi.org/10.1016/j.amjmed.2015.01.033.

Osório, Flávia de L., et al. "Antidepressant Effects of a Single Dose of Ayahuasca in Patients with Recurrent Depression: A Preliminary Report." *Brazilian Journal of Psychiatry* 37, no. 1 (2015): 13–20. http://doi.org/10.1590/1516-4446-2014-1496.

Ott, Jonathan. *Ayahuasca Analogues: Pangaean Entheogens.* Kennewick, WA: Natural Products, 1994.

Oyuela-Caycedo, Augusto, and Nicholas C. Kawa. "A Deep History of Tobacco in Lowland South America." In *The Master Plant: Tobacco in Lowland South America*, edited by Andrew Russell and Elizabeth Rahman, 27–44. London: Bloomsbury Academic, 2015.

Palhano-Fontes, F., et al. "Rapid Antidepressant Effects of the Psyche- delic Ayahuasca in Treatment-Resistant Depression: A Randomized Placebo-Controlled Trial." *Psychological Medicine* 49, no. 4 (2019): 655–63. http://doi.org/10.1017/S0033291718001356.

Papke, Roger L. "Merging Old and New Perspectives on Nicotinic Acetyl- choline Receptors." *Biochemical Pharmacology* 89, no. 1 (2014): 1–11. http://doi.org/10.1016/j.bcp.2014.01.029.

Park, Hae-Ryung, et al. "Transcriptional Response of Primary Human Airway Epithelial Cells to Flavoring Chemicals in Electronic Cigarettes." *Scientific Reports* 9 (2018): 1400. http://doi.org/10.1038/s41598-018-37913-9.

Patanavanich, Roengrudee, and Stanton A. Glantz. "Smoking Is Associated with COVID-19 Progression: A Meta-analysis." *Nicotine & Tobacco Research* (2020): 1–4. http://doi.org/10.1093/ntr/ntaa082.

Peluso, Daniela. "Ayahuasca's Attractions and Distractions: Examining Sexual Seduction in Shaman-Participant Interactions." In *Ayahuasca Shamanism in the Amazon and Beyond*, edited by Beatriz Caiuby Labate and Clancy Canvar, 231–55. Oxford: Oxford University Press, 2014.

Pendell, Dale. *Pharmako/poeia: Plant Powers, Poisons, and Herbcraft*. San Francisco: Mercury House, 1995.

Perlman, David. "Nicotine Study Surprises Scientists." *The Brain in the News* (July 13, 2001): 1, 3.

Politi, Matteo. "Drinking Ayahuasca without DMT Is Powerful and Traditional." 2020. https://kahpi.net/ayahuasca-vine-only-without-dmt-banisteriopsis-caapi.

Politi, Matteo, et al. "Traditional Use of *Banisteriopsis caapi* Alone and Its Application in a Context of Drug Addiction Therapy." *Journal of Psychoactive Drugs* (2020). http://doi.org/10.1080/02791072.2020.1820641.

Pollan, Michael. *How to Change Your Mind: What the New Science of Psychedelics Teaches Us about Consciousness, Dying, Addiction, Depression and Transcendence*. New York: Penguin Press, 2018.

Prickett, James L., and Mitchell B. Liester. "Hypotheses Regarding Ayahuasca's Potential Mechanisms of Action in the Treatment of Addiction." In *The Therapeutic Use of Ayahuasca*, edited by Beatriz C. Labate and Clancy Cavnar, 111–32. Berlin: Springer, 2014.

Quik, Maryka, et al. "Nicotine and Parkinson's Disease: Implications for Therapy." *Movement Disorders* 23, no. 12 (2008): 1641–52. http://doi.org/10.1002/mds.21900.

Rätsch, Christian. *The Encyclopedia of Psychoactive Plants: Ethnopharmacology and Its Applications*. Rochester, VT: Park Street Press, 2005.

Reichel-Dolmatoff, Gerardo. *Amazonian Cosmos: The Sexual and Religious Symbolism of the Tukano Indians.* Chicago: University of Chicago Press, 1971.

———. "The Cultural Context of an Aboriginal Hallucinogen: *Banisteriopsis caapi.*" In *Flesh of the Gods: The Ritual Use of Hallucinogens,* edited by Peter T. Furst, 84–113. New York: Praeger, 1972.

———. *The Shaman and the Jaguar: A Study of Narcotic Drugs among the Indians of Colombia.* Philadelphia: Temple University Press, 1975.

Riba, Jordi, et al. "Effects of the South American Psychoactive Beverage Ayahuasca on Regional Brain Electrical Activity in Humans: A Functional Neuroimaging Study Using Low-Resolution Electromagnetic Tomography." *Neuropsychobiology* 50 (2004): 89–101. http://doi.org/10.1159/000077946.

Rivier, Laurent, and Jan-Erik Lindgren. "'Ayahuasca,' the South American Hallucinogenic Drink: An Ethnobotanical and Chemical Investigation." *Economic Botany* 26 (1972): 101–29.

Rostron, Brian L., et al. "Smokeless Tobacco Use and Circulatory Disease Risk: A Systematic Review and Meta-analysis." *Open Heart* 5 (2018): e000846. http://doi.org/10.1136/epenhrt-2018-000846.

Rudgley, Richard. *The Encyclopedia of Psychoactive Substances.* New York: St. Martin's, 2014. First published 1998 by Little, Brown.

Sanches, Rafael Faria, et al. "Antidepressant Effects of a Single Dose of Ayahuasca in Patients with Recurrent Depression." *Journal of Clinical Psychopharmacology* 36, no. 1 (2016): 77–81. http://doi.org/10.1097/JCP0000000000000436.

Schenberg, Eduardo Ekman, et al. "Acute Biphasic Effects of Ayahuasca." *PLOS ONE* 10, no. 9 (2015): e0137202. http://doi.org/10.1371/journal.pone.0137202.

Schultes, Richard Evans. "Avenues for Future Ethnobotanical Research into New World Hallucinogens and Their Uses." In *Drugs, Rituals, and Altered States of Consciousness,* edited by Brian M. Du Toit, 261–67. Rotterdam: A. A. Balkena, 1977.

———. "Recognition of Variability in Wild Plants by Indians of the

Northwest Amazon: An Enigma." *Journal of Ethnobiology* 6, no. 2 (1986): 229–38.

Schwarz, M. J., et al. "Activities of Extract and Constituents of *Banisteriopsis caapi* Relevant to Parkinsonism." *Pharmacology Biochemistry and Behaviour* 75, no. 3 (2003): 627–33. http://doi.org/10.1016/S0091 -3057(03)00129-1.

Shanon, Benny. *The Antipodes of the Mind: Charting the Phenomenology of the Ayahuasca Experience*. Oxford: Oxford University Press, 2002.

Sheldrake, Merlin. "The 'Enigma' of Richard Schultes, Amazonian Hallucinogenic Plants, and the Limits of Ethnobotany." *Social Studies of Science* 50, no. 3 (2020): 345–76. http://doi.org/10.1177/03063 12720920362.

Shepard, Glenn H. "Psychoactive Plants and Ethnopsychiatric Medicines of the Matsigenka." *Journal of Psychoactive Drugs* 30, no. 4 (1998): 321–32.

Shiels, Meredith S., et al. "Association of Cigarette Smoking, Alcohol Consumption, and Physical Activity with Sex Steroid Hormone Levels in US Men." *Cancer Causes Control* 20, no. 6 (2009): 877–86. http://doi .org/10.1007/s10552-009-9318-y.

Shulgin, Alexander, and Ann Shulgin. *TIHKAL: The Continuation*. Berkeley: Transform Press, 1997.

Sisson, Verne A., and R. F. Severson. "Alkaloid Composition of the *Nicotiana* Species." *Beiträge zur Tabakforschung International* 14, no. 6 (1990): 327–39. http://doi.org/10.2478/cttr-2013-0610.

Spinella, Marcello. *The Pharmacology of Herbal Medicine: Plant Drugs that Alter Mind, Brain, and Behavior*. Cambridge, MA: MIT Press, 2001.

Spruce, Richard. "On Some Remarkable Narcotics of the Amazon Valley and Orinoco." *Geographical Magazine* 1 (1874): 184–93.

Stanfill, Stephen B., et al. "Comprehensive Chemical Characterization of *Rapé* Tobacco Products: Nicotine, Un-ionized Nicotine, Tobacco-Specific N'-Nitrosamines, Polycyclic Aromatic Hydrocarbons, and Flavor Constituents." *Food and Chemical Toxicology* 82 (2015): 50–58. http://doi.org/10.1016/j.fct.2015.04.016.

Sterne, Jonathan A. C., et al. "Association between Administration of Systemic Corticosteroids and Mortality among Critically Ill Patients with Covid-19: A Meta-analysis." *Journal of the American Medical Association*. Published online September 2, 2020. http://doi.org/10.1001/jama.2020.17023.

Sun, Bo, et al. "Variations of Alkaloid Accumulation and Gene Transcription in *Nicotiana tabacum*." *Biomolecules* 8, no. 4 (2018): 114. http://doi.org/10.3390/biom8040114.

Szabo, Attila, et al. "The Endogenous Hallucinogen and Trace Amine N,N-Dimethyltryptamine (DMT) Displays Potent Protective Effects against Hypoxia via Sigma-1 Receptor Activation in Human Primary IPSC-Derived Cortical Neurons and Microglia-like Immune Cells." *Frontiers in Neuroscience* 10, article 423 (2016). http://doi.org/10.3389/fnins.2016.00423.

Taghavi, Sahar, et al. "Nicotine Content of Domestic Cigarettes, Imported Cigarettes, and Pipe Tobacco in Iran." *Addiction & Health* 4, no. 12 (2012): 28–35.

Talin, Piera, and Emilia Sanabria. "Ayahuasca's Entwined Efficacy: An Ethnographic Study of Ritual Healing from 'Addiction.'" *International Journal of Drug Policy* 44 (2017): 23–30. http://doi.org/10.1016/j.drugpo.2017.02.017.

Tchounwou, Paul B., et al. "Heavy Metals Toxicity and the Environment." In *Molecular, Clinical, and Environmental Toxicology*, Experientia Supplementum, vol. 101, edited by A. Luch, 133–64. Basel: Springer, 2012. http://doi.org/10.1007/978-3-7643-8340-4_6.

Tindle, Hilary A., et al. "Beyond Smoking Cessation: Investigating Medicinal Nicotine to Prevent and Treat COVID-19." *Nicotine & Tobacco Research* (2020): 1669–70. http://doi.org/10.1093/ntr/ntaa077.

Torres, Constantino Manuel. "The Origin of the Ayahuasca/Yagé Concept: An Inquiry into the Synergy between Dimethyltryptamine and Beta-Carbolines." In *Ancient Psychoactive Substances*, edited by Scott M. Fitzpatrick, 234–64. Gainesville: University Press of Florida, 2018.

Travis, Ruth C., and Timothy J. Key. "Oestrogen Exposure and Breast

Cancer Risk." *Breast Cancer Research* 5 (2003): 239–47. http://doi
.org/10.1186/bcr628.

Tresca, Giorgia, et al. "Evaluating Herbal Medicine Preparation from
a Traditional Perspective: Insights from an Ethnopharmaceutical
Survey in the Peruvian Amazon." *Anthropology & Medicine* 27, no. 3
(2020): 268–84. http://doi.org/10.1080/13648470.2019.1669939.

Trimarchi, Maria, and Ann Meeker-O'Connell. "How Nicotine Works."
HowStuffWorks.com, January 2, 2001. https://science.howstuffworks
.com/nicotine.htm.

Tupper, Kenneth W., and Beatriz Caiuby Labate. "Ayahuasca, Psychedelic
Studies, and Health Sciences: The Politics of Knowledge and Inquiry
into an Amazonian Plant Brew." *Current Drug Abuse Reviews* 7, no. 2
(2014): 71–80. http://doi.org/10.2174/1874473708666150107155042.

Ujváry, István. "Nicotine and Other Insecticidal Alkaloids." In *Nicotinoid
Insecticides and the Nicotinic Acetylcholine Receptor*, edited by Izuru
Yamamoto and John E. Casida, 29–69. Tokyo: Springer-Verlag, 1999.

Unger, Michael, and Darian W. Unger. "E-Cigarettes / Electronic Nicotine
Delivery Systems: A Word of Caution on Health and New Prod-
uct Development." *Journal of Thoracic Disease* 10, suppl. 22 (2018):
S2588–92. http://doi.org/10.21037/jtd.2018.07.99.

US Food and Drug Administration. "Some E-Cigarette Users Are Having
Seizures, Most Reports Involving Youth and Young Adults." Special
announcement, April 10, 2019.

Usman, Muhammad Shariq, et al. "Is There a Smoker's Paradox in
COVID-19?" *BMJ Evidence-Based Medicine* (first published online
August 11, 2020). http://doi.org/10.1136/bmjebm-2020-111492.

Uthaug, M. V., et al. "Sub-acute and Long-Term Effects of Ayahuasca on
Affect and Cognitive Thinking Style and Their Association with Ego
Dissolution." *Psychopharmacology* 235 (2018): 2979–89. http://doi
.org/10.1007/s00213-018-4988-3.

Valentine, Gerald, and Mehmet Sofuoglu. "Cognitive Effects of Nicotine:
Recent Progress." *Current Neuropharmacology* 16 (2018): 403–14.
http://doi.org/10.2174/1570159X15666171103152136.

Velasquez-Manoff, Moises. "How Covid Sends Some Bodies to War with Themselves." *New York Times Magazine* (August 11, 2020).

Viol, A., et al. "Shannon Entropy of Brain Functional Complex Networks under the Influence of the Psychedelic Ayahuasca." *Scientific Reports* 7. http://doi.org/10.1038/s41598-017-06854-0.

Viveiros de Castro, Eduardo. "Perspectivism and Multinaturalism in Indigenous America." In *The land Within: Indigenous Territory and the Perception of Environment*, edited by Alexandre Surrallés and Pedro García Hierro, 36–74. Copenhagen: IWGIA, 2005.

———. "The Relative Native." *HAU: Journal of Ethnographic Theory* 3, no. 3 (2013): 473–502.

Wang, Qixin, et al. "E-Cigarette-Induced Pulmonary Inflammation and Dysregulated Repair Are Mediated by nAChR α7 Receptor: Role of nAChR α7 in SARS-CoV-2 Covid-19 ACE2 Receptor Regulation." *Respiratory Research* 21 (2020): 154. http://doi.org/10.1186/s12931-020 -01396-y.

Wang, Wei, et al. "Cigarette Smoking Has a Positive and Independent Effect on Testosterone Levels." *Hormones* 12, no. 4 (2013): 567–77. http://doi.org/10.14310/horm.2002.1445.

Wang, Yan-Hong, et al. "Composition, Standardization, and Chemical Profiling of *Banisteriopsis caapi*, a Plant for the Treatment of Neurodegenerative Disorders Relevant to Parkinson's Disease." *Journal of Ethnopharmacology* 128, no. 3 (2010): 662–71. http://doi.org/10.1016/j .jep.2010.02.013.

Weiskopf, Jimmy. *Yajé, the New Purgatory: Encounters with Ayahuasca*. Bogotá: Villegas Editores, 2005.

Wessler, Ignaz, and Charles James Kirkpatrick. "Acetylcholine beyond Neurons: The Non-neuronal Cholinergic System in Humans." *British Journal of Pharmacology* 154 (2008): 1558–71. http://doi.org/10.1038 /bjp.2008.185.

Wessler, Ignaz, et al. "The Non-neuronal Cholinergic System: The Biological Role of Non-neuronal Acetylcholine in Plants and Humans." *Japanese Journal of Pharmacology* 85, no. 1 (2001): 2–10.

Whitten, Norman E., Jr. *Sacha Runa: Ethnicity and Adaptation of Ecuadorian Jungle Quichua*. Urbana: University of Illinois Press, 1976.

Wilbert, Johannes. *Tobacco and Shamanism in South America*. New Haven: Yale University Press, 1987.

———. "Does Pharmacology Corroborate the Nicotine Therapy and Practices of South American Shamanism?" *Journal of Ethnopharmacology* 32 (1991): 179–86.

Wu, Katherine J. "Vaping Links to Covid-19 Risk Are Becoming Clear." *New York Times International Edition* (September 8, 2020): 6.

Wu, Weijia, et al. "Determination of Carcinogenic Tobacco-Specific Nitrosamines in Mainstream Smoke from US-Brand and Non-US-Brand Cigarettes from 14 Countries." *Nicotine & Tobacco Research* 7, no. 3 (2005): 443–51. http://doi.org/10.1080/14622200500125898.

Wyss, Annah B., et al. "Smokeless Tobacco Use and the Risk of Head and Neck Cancer: Pooled Analysis of US Studies in the INHANCE Consortium." *American Journal of Epidemiology* 184, no. 10 (2016): 703–16. http://doi.org/10.1093/aje/kww075.

Zemkova, Hana, et al. "Multiple Cholinergic Signaling Pathways in Pituitary Gonadotrophs." *Endocrinology* 154, no. 1 (2013): 421–33. http://doi.org/10.1210/en.2012-1554.

Zhu, Shu-Hong, et al. "Four Hundred and Sixty Brands of E-Cigarettes and Counting: Implications for Product Regulation." *Tobacco Control* 23 (2014): iii3–9. http://doi.org/10.1136/tobaccocontrol-2014-051670.

INDEX

ABOUT THE AUTHORS

Jeremy Narby was born in 1959 in Montreal, Canada. He studied history at the University of Kent at Canterbury and obtained a doctorate in anthropology from Stanford University. He spent several years living with Asháninka people in the Peruvian Amazon, cataloging indigenous uses of rainforest resources. Since 1990, he has worked for a humanitarian organization based in Switzerland, Nouvelle Planète, fundraising for the initiatives of indigenous Amazonian people to gain land rights, to set up bilingual education programs, and to protect the rainforest from destruction and contamination. He has written several books about the knowledge of Amazonian people, including *The Cosmic Serpent*, which have been translated into a total of seventeen languages.

Rafael Chanchari Pizuri was born in 1962 in an indigenous community called Chacatán in the province of Datem del Marañón in the Loreto region of Peru. For the first fifteen years of his life, he spoke only his mother tongue, Shawi. Then he went to school and learned Spanish. He became so proficient that he was selected to teach Spanish to other Shawi people. Several years later, a newly founded bilingual education program for indigenous people came looking for a Shawi person who could teach in the Shawi language; and so, at age thirty-two, Rafael Chanchari went to Iquitos, 450 kilometers from his homeland, to teach young Shawi teachers-in-training about their own language and culture. To this day, he lives in Iquitos and continues to work as a teacher of indigenous teachers. Along the way, he also became a *médico*, a specialist who heals people with indigenous medicine. He tends to a large garden of medicinal plants not far from Iquitos.